GOD SENT A MAN

Carlyle B. Haynes

REVIEW AND HERALD® PUBLISHING ASSOCIATION

Since 1861 | www.reviewandherald.com

Additional copies of this book can be obtained by calling toll-free
1-800-765-6955 or by visiting http://www.adventistbookcenter.com.

ISBN 978-0-8280-1271-3

May 2016

Table of Contents

Foreword

When you open a book you are entitled to learn from its title and table of contents something of what you are about to read. You deserve a clear and definite idea of the purpose and aim of the writer.

It is not easy to compress the whole purpose and theme of a book within its title and chapter heads. Consequently, I am using this Foreword to let you know at the outset what I have in mind to accomplish by this book.

It is in my mind to produce in your mind a profound and unshakable conviction that will alter your whole outlook on life and provide you with a philosophy that will transform your life from a meaningless conglomeration of fortuitous changes into a meaningful and divinely arranged plan.

I would have you believe that the universe and everything in it, including every person and the whole of each person's environment, with every event, every occurrence, every occasion, both good and bad, together with all human history, its wars, its victories and defeats, its developments and changes, its dynasties and reigns, are in the hands and under the control of a beneficent God; and that "in everything God works for good with those who love him, who are called according to his purpose."

This is what I would have you believe. And I would have you include in this belief the knowledge that this providential supervision of each life, as well as of all history, takes in your personal life and its concerns and affairs and interests and welfare. Your times are in God's hands. Moreover, it is possible for you to be so in harmony with the Will that controls and orders the universe, and the most insignificant atom in it, that your life may follow its prescribed and prearranged course, and fulfill in every detail the purpose and plan God has, and is working out, for you.

No man can live a life that is so full, so content, so assured, so secure, so satisfying, as the man who accepts and carries into action such a conviction. If you once believe that a good and all-powerful God has shaped a plan for your life, and is quite able to carry it out if you will bring yourself into harmony with His will, and believe it fully enough to rely on it under all circumstances, and allow nothing to shake your conviction in God's superintending providence for you, your whole outlook on life, on history, on current events, and on your environment will be so changed as

5

to bring to you the most satisfying and most abundant life any man can ever live.

To produce this conviction in your mind and belief, I propose only to spread before you the narrative of a life—a life the account of which, told in an ancient sheaf of manuscripts, constitutes the most fascinating and impressive tale in the literature of humanity. This is the story of Joseph, son of Jacob.

If it means anything to you to arrive at a firm conviction, which will undergird your entire life, that men and nations are in God's hand, that He does according to His will among the people of earth, that "in everything God works for good with those who love him," that those who follow Him are not now or ever the helpless victims of environment or circumstances, that circumstances can always be turned into providences because God uses circumstances to bring about His own overruling purpose, that you can have a life and live a life in which nothing goes wrong, and in which all the disciplines of life are allowed to shape and mold you into the person God has in mind to make, made after His own image, in complete harmony with His all-ruling will—then read on.

THE AUTHOR

CHAPTER 1

At Hebron

THERE was something impressive about the scene, about the widely spreading black goatskin tents pitched on the open plains. There were two camps, with a considerable distance between, and scores of shaggy tent dwellings ranged around the larger and more elaborate dwelling of the chieftains of the respective clans. Spread out from each encampment at great distances were grazing flocks and herds.

In front of the many-roomed and widely spread central tabernacle of one of the chieftains were two figures, an old man and a youth. The old man was seated; the boy was standing at his knee. The boy was looking earnestly into the face of the old man, listening intently to the narrative that his grandfather was relating to him.

The lad had come from the other encampment, which was his own home, belonging to his father. During past weeks he had traversed the distance between the two camps many times, and always with eagerness to hear another tale of his people that his grandfather delighted to tell him. These stories, of which the old man seemed to have an endless supply, moved the lad deeply. They disclosed to him the existence of a God, the only true God, the Maker of all things, who had chosen his great-grandfather, Abraham, and had chosen his clan, his line, for a high destiny in the affairs of men. This knowledge of the existence of an all-knowing God, the greatest fact in the universe, came to this lad in his early years, and it came with enormous impact upon his maturing mind.

Isaac and Joseph

The old man, long a dweller in this land, was named Isaac, son of Abraham. The boy, a newcomer in this vicinity, was named Joseph, son of Jacob, who in turn was Isaac's son.

7

At the time we make their acquaintance Isaac was 163 years of age, Jacob 103, Joseph 12.

Joseph had been born in a distant land, Padan-aram. His mother, who was a native of Padan-aram, had died on the journey from her homeland to that of Jacob. Jacob had been away from his early home for more than twenty years, and had gained great wealth in flocks and herds during that time, together with a large, boisterous family. Joseph was next to the youngest child in that family.

Joseph had known his grandfather only a short time, but in that brief period he had come to love him with a deep and tender affection.

He liked nothing better than to visit Grandfather Isaac and drink in the absorbing narratives that Isaac took great satisfaction in relating to him. Isaac had little to occupy his time, and he was delighted to have this sturdy and likable lad visit him.

Isaac was not only old, he was also blind. His mind, however, was alert, and he loved to send it roving down the long corridors of the past, dwelling upon the great experiences of his long life, and the way in which the God of his father Abraham had dealt with him.

Building Character

Joseph's father, Jacob, recently renamed Israel after his long exile in Padan-aram, had returned to Canaan, and had sought and gained a reconciliation with his brother Esau, with whom a family breach had existed for more than a score of years. From Penuel, where the reconciliation had taken place, and in possession of his new name and new nature, Israel journeyed first to Succoth and then on to Shechem. It was apparently his purpose to settle at Shechem, inasmuch as he bought a piece of ground.

His purpose, however, was frustrated by the treachery of his sons, Simeon and Levi, in the matter of his daughter Dinah. This resulted in his being driven from that beautiful and fruitful valley. Under the direction of God he went first to Bethel, where the beloved Rachel, Joseph's mother, died in giving birth to Benjamin. Afterward Israel journeyed southward to Hebron, where his father Isaac still lived. He established his permanent encampment, with all his flocks and herds, only a short distance from that of Isaac.

Thus Joseph came to know his grandfather.

8

AT HEBRON

The path between the two encampments of father and son, Isaac and Israel, soon became a well-traveled one for Joseph. Something about his grandfather's narratives always moved him deeply with a sense of destiny, first of the glorious future promised his family and later that something of more-than-ordinary importance would shape and mold his own life.

Isaac too was aware of this sense of something out of the ordinary in the future of this lad whom he loved. It was this that impelled him to choose with care the stories he related to this eager lad, and to endeavor to convey to him the lessons, always big with importance, that they contained.

The stories that particularly pleased Joseph were those about his great-grandfather Abraham, the noble patriarch and progenitor of his line. And it was these stories that Isaac loved most to tell.

CHAPTER 2

Toward Moriah's Land

LET us in imagination sit with Joseph as Isaac relates the most exciting and moving tale he had yet told the boy, a narrative of his own deliverance from death at the hands of the father who loved him. Nothing before had so stirred the deepest feelings of Joseph's soul. He relived it all as Isaac told it, and his love and admiration for the old man were immeasurably enlarged.

God, the one true God, the great and awesome Jehovah, Isaac said, chose Abraham and brought him from his own country, Ur of the Chaldees, and led him to Canaan, which He promised should be his and his descendants' in perpetuity. Abraham believed God, and became so close to God that he became known as "the friend of God." God made Himself known to him, talked with him, made him astonishing and glorious promises of a grand future for himself and his children. In all of this, great emphasis again and again was placed upon "the seed of Abraham." Abraham was to have a "seed," and it was through this "seed" that all the glorious promises of the future were to be brought about. Again and again Jehovah renewed these promises.

Even before Isaac was born the promise was made that Abraham's seed were to be as numerous as the stars of heaven and would bring blessing to all the nations of earth. After the birth of Isaac, Jehovah declared, "In Isaac shall thy seed be called." More than that, God declared over and over, "My covenant will I establish with Isaac."

In the birth of Isaac his son, and in the promises concerning him, Abraham had taken great comfort and experienced great joy. All this Abraham had told Isaac as he grew toward manhood. Abraham told him of the promises God had made regarding him, told him too of the faith of his mother, Sarah, and of the stupendous miracle that had brought

Isaac into being. Abraham made it plain that all his hopes of the future centered in Isaac. His affection, his interest, his confidence, his dearest expectations—all were summed up in this boy of his.

Abraham Tested

When Isaac was still a young man God spoke to Abraham, calling him by name. Abraham was familiar with Jehovah's voice. Consequently, when God said to him, "Abraham," no doubt shadowed Abraham's mind. He knew it was God speaking to him. He replied, "Yes, Lord, I am here."

Without any question, it was Jehovah who was speaking to Abraham. But what a shattering, bewildering, wholly unaccountable command it was that now came from the divine voice! And what a tumult of confusion it must have produced in the mind and heart and affections of the old man.

"Take now thy son, thine only son Isaac, whom thou lovest, and get thee into the land of Moriah; and offer him there for a burnt offering upon one of the mountains which I will tell thee of."

There was no mistaking the meaning of the command. The one to be taken was named. It was Isaac. The land to be visited was specified. It was Moriah. What was to be done to Isaac was clear. He was to be offered as a burnt offering.

That meant only one thing for Isaac—death! And this before any of the grand promises could possibly be realized. Isaac had no son.

Abraham was stunned. Had not God said, "In Isaac shall thy seed be called"? What could God now mean by ordering him to take this son, through whom alone God's promises could be fulfilled, and offer him as a sacrifice? With Isaac dead there could be no seed!

In relating the story Isaac made it plain to Joseph that he had known nothing of this at the time. Only Abraham knew. And it must have appalled him. But he did not stop to deal with the questions that deluged his mind. God had spoken, the God who had made all the promises, the God who had led him all his life, the God who by a miracle had given him Isaac. There was but one thing to do when God spoke. God's word was sufficient and final. Moreover, there must be no delay, no waiting for explanation or more light. The command was "Take *now* thy son."

Instantly Abraham obeyed, still saying nothing to his son. The heavy-hearted father "rose up early in the morning, and saddled his ass, . . . and clave the wood for the burnt offering, and rose up, and went unto the place of which God had told him."

Importance of Instant Obedience

Joseph could not have learned in any more vivid and impressive way of the importance of instant obedience to the voice of God. He must have held his breath as Isaac related the details. "God said to my father, 'Get thee into the land.' My father 'rose up early . . . and went.'

"I was delighted to go with my father. I enjoyed being with him. He told me nothing of the purpose of this journey. Nor did he tell the two servants anything. They must have realized, from the wood for the burnt offering and the fire we took, that there was to be a sacrifice. But what was to be sacrificed they did not know. Nor did I. You see, my dear boy, we had no idea what was going on in father's heart. Faith is a personal thing. It cannot be transferred to others nor left as a legacy. It involves a personal relationship to the invisible and Almighty Jehovah. No person can have faith for some friend or relative. God was dealing with my father."

Three days were required to cover the distance to Moriah. Those days provided an opportunity for Abraham to resolve the turbulence of his mind and heart and to reflect, with what calmness he could muster, on this act of his in taking his son to Moriah to sacrifice. How could he possibly kill this beautiful son in whom all his hopes were centered? What sort of life could he live afterward?

Joseph was listening with rapt attention to the words of his grandfather. He was not only profoundly interested in the story of his ancestor, "the friend of God," but he was also learning lessons of the greatest worth, lessons that formed the foundation of his education and made him the great figure he afterward became. He did not realize it at the time, but his character was in process of formation as he drank in these thrilling tales told him by Isaac.

Lessons Joseph Learned

In the story of the sacrifice of Isaac, Joseph learned the importance of implicit faith in God and of instant obedience that required no reasons, no explanation from God. And these lessons he learned for all his life that was to follow. He did not need to learn them again.

Isaac proceeded with his story of the great experience of his life. The journey to Moriah took three days. He was conscious on the first day that his father was studying him closely. He saw the old man's eyes upon him many times during the day. His father was strangely uncommunicative. Abraham loved his son. He was not only the son of his old age, long and earnestly wanted; he was also Abraham's hope for all the future promises of God for the great destiny of his family. As they tramped along on their way to Moriah, Abraham furtively watched Isaac. He observed his expressions, his carefree happiness at being along on this journey. Oh, how he loved this dear lad God had given him!

The old man knew he would need to tell Isaac that God, the great Jehovah, had given a command that he should be killed, and that he, Abraham, must do it. This turned his mind to the many times he had told this boy, with great joy and eager hope, of the great promises of God. Would he now have to find some reasons why God was going back on His promises? What were those reasons? He did not know. He knew only what God had told him to do—and one other thing: he knew God!

Since God had told him to take Isaac to Moriah and offer him up, Abraham was conscious that his already great love for Isaac had enlarged immeasurably. It nearly smothered him. Never before had he realized how much he loved this boy of his. Nevertheless, he kept his face steadily toward Moriah's land. The God he served must be obeyed.

Without doubt, on the second day of the journey Abraham's mind turned to the servants who accompanied them. What did he need to tell them concerning this human sacrifice? What attitude would they take toward it if they knew? They could prevent it by force if they would. He must not tell them. The sacrifice must be made. God had spoken.

And Isaac himself! He was a strong, vigorous youth. Abraham was old. Isaac could resist, and no doubt could prevent his father from taking his life. Isaac must not be told—at any rate until the last moment. God's will must be done. Abraham had not the least doubt. He kept his face steadfastly toward Moriah.

Leaving the Irreconcilable to God

And so the third day came, and they pressed on to their destination. Now the contradiction between what God had promised him and what God now ordered him to do became dreadfully acute in Abraham's mind.

How could Isaac be the seed and also be dead? There was no reconciling the two. Abraham gave up trying to solve it, and simply left it in the hands—the capable hands, the infinite hands, the almighty hands—of the God he loved and trusted—and went on to Moriah.

And when he arrived there it was with a clear mind and trustful heart. He knew the answer now. He disclosed that knowledge when he said to the servants, "Abide ye here with the ass; and I and the lad will go yonder and worship, and come again to you." He did not say that to hide anything from them, to deceive them. He said it because he believed it. He and the lad would come again to them.

How could that be when he was going to kill the boy? How could they then both come back? No, Abraham was not lying. He spoke words of truth and soberness. He spoke words of great faith. He believed they both would come back. For Abraham at last had the contradiction solved. The problem that had so tortured his mind was not after all his problem. It was God's problem. God had told him to kill his son. But God had also given him the promises about Isaac. God had spoken twice, the second time contradicting the first. Very well, God would find the solution. And Abraham would leave it with Him. And he thought he knew now how God would do it. He would do it by raising Isaac from the dead. But Abraham would leave it with God. That was God's part. His own part was to do what God told him to do.

That this was the solution at which Abraham had arrived in his own mind is made plain in Hebrews 11:17-19:

"By faith Abraham, when he was tried, offered up Isaac: and he that had received the promises offered up his only begotten son, of whom it was said, That in Isaac shall thy seed be called: accounting that God was able to raise him up, even from the dead; from whence also he received him in a figure."

14

CHAPTER 3

Deliverance From Death

WITH the deepest eagerness Joseph anticipated his next visit with his grandfather. He had been compelled to leave on the former occasion before the completion of Isaac's narrative, because the shadows of twilight had begun to fall around them and there were duties he was expected to perform at the encampment of his father.

Through the hours that passed while he was at home his mind was occupied with the experiences of Isaac's great adventure. He heard again the dread and totally unexpected command of the God of Abraham for him to take his son, Isaac, and offer him as a sacrifice on Moriah's summit. He saw again the instant, unhesitating obedience of the patriarch. And the impression in his heart and mind deepened regarding the way of faith, and the importance of implicit, unquestioning obedience, as well as the necessity always of being in harmony with the divine will. Deeply he pondered these things, and the lessons they conveyed became fixed and permanent principles of his life.

When the opportunity came to return to Isaac he hurried along the trail eagerly. He found Isaac in his customary place, motionlessly looking out into a world that he did not see, yet living in a world unseen by others but quite real to himself. He greeted his grandson with quiet pleasure, and was immediately pressed by Joseph to carry on with the tale of the great experience of his life.

As they left the servants to continue on alone for the remainder of the journey, Isaac said, Abraham took the wood and laid it upon Isaac, the wood upon which Isaac before long was to be laid as a sacrifice, but about which Isaac for the moment knew nothing. Abraham "took the fire in his hand, and a knife." Then the two of them, the old man and the sturdy youth, journeyed on together to the top of Moriah.

15

Abraham's Hardest Task

Abraham must have known, of course, Isaac explained, that the time must come when he would find it necessary to disclose to his son that God had designated Isaac as the victim of the sacrifice. He must have dreaded that moment. He put it off as long as he could, indeed, until he could put it off no longer. It is plain that Abraham faced the hardest task that had ever confronted him. This son whom he cherished, whom he loved above all things on earth, in whom were centered all his hopes of realizing the glorious promises of God, he was now with his own hand to slay. He was to destroy with his own hand all that made life valuable to him.

Moreover, as he did this, he was to love and worship the One who commanded the sacrifice. He was required to explain to Isaac, whom he had taught to look forward to the fairest, happiest life, that he must now take that life. He was to contradict all he had ever told Isaac. He was now to tell him that he was grown to manhood only to be cut down by his own father in the very prime of life, in the very hope of his opening manhood. Oh, the tumult of thoughts that must have raced through the tortured mind of Abraham as they tramped on up the slopes of Moriah.

Possibly the thought would come to him that God was now recalling the great gift He had made. And perhaps it was because of some failure, some weakness, some fault, some sin of his own. He must have passed his whole life in review before his searching, groping mind. Where had he been at fault? Was his son to die because in some unwitting way Abraham had sinned against God?

It was a tragic journey up Moriah's side. It would have been no surprise if in this horror of great darkness Abraham's mind had become unhinged and unbalanced. It would have been no wonder if he had taken his own life in order to make impossible the taking of Isaac's life. He might have reasoned that nothing that could befall him if he disobeyed God could exceed the pain and the agony of obedience.

Young as Joseph was, he caught some idea of the supreme trial this experience must have been to Abraham, and his admiration and love for his great ancestor grew enormously. He began to see, too, that though Abraham was the hero in this trying scene, there was also another actor in it who passed through almost as great a trial. It was plain that to Isaac this was the memorable, the outstanding, day of his life. Quiet and serene as he was by nature, every faculty must have now been stirred and strained

16

to the utmost. While Abraham could not find it in his heart to disclose to his son the object of this journey, and continued even to the last to keep Isaac in ignorance of the part he was to play, the boy was becoming more and more conscious that there was something going forward that was mysterious and undisclosed. He was aware that Abraham watched him closely. He was aware, too, that he himself was tensely watching his father. "And so," the record declares, and declares twice over, "they went both of them together."

Yes, Isaac continued, they went on together, but with minds how differently occupied! The father's heart was torn with anguish, distracted by a thousand thoughts. The son's mind, quite disengaged and occupied up to this time only with new scenes and passing fancies, now began to be aware of the strangeness and tenseness of his father.

It was not long before Isaac hazarded speech. They were approaching the summit of the mountain. Isaac was struck by the silent and sober demeanor of his father. He feared it might have been through absence of mind that he had neglected to bring the lamb. He ventured to attract his father's attention to this.

"My father."

"Yes, my son."

"We have brought fire and wood. But where is the lamb for a burnt offering?"

It was the moment Abraham had dreaded. Nevertheless, his strong heart bore up calmly and his humble faith helped him to reply:

"My son, God will provide himself a lamb for a burnt offering."

The Sacrifice—Isaac

Abraham realized that the terrible truth could be hidden from Isaac no longer. But still he put it off while he busied himself gathering stones to make an altar. "The Lord will provide . . . a lamb." That is what he said to Isaac. And that was what he believed. But Isaac did not know that in his father's mind the Lord had already provided Himself a lamb, and that the lamb was Isaac.

How would Abraham go about his dreaded task? The stones of the altar were laid. There could be delay no longer. How would Abraham say what must be said? Would he draw back? Would he weaken? Would he break down? He busied himself with arranging the wood on the altar. And he thought, yes, the Lord will provide, has provided, Himself, with a lamb. He has fixed upon my son. He is God's sacrifice. Well, Isaac belonged to God. There would have been no Isaac, could have been no Isaac, except as God gave him being. So God could rightly do as He pleased with Isaac. If it pleased Him to make Isaac a lamb, He could do so. God owned Isaac. Abraham was steward, not owner, of his son. That is true of all parents. It was true in a special way of Abraham.

There was now no other thing for Abraham to do to delay telling Isaac. The altar was finished, the wood in order upon it. Everything was in readiness for the sacrifice, everything but Isaac. He must now be told of God's plan.

With a tenderness that no words can describe, Abraham told his son what God had commanded him to do. Isaac was to be the sacrifice. Before the lad could utter a remonstrance, or recover from the shock of his surprise, the father reminded him of his miraculous birth in answer to prayer; pointed out that he had his being from God and belonged to God; declared to him God's right to take away, in any manner He pleased, the gift He had bestowed. He told him, too, what a blessing and comfort he had been to Sarah and to himself, how deeply they loved him, how fondly they had centered their hopes upon him, and what a crushing, shattering thing this command of God had been to him. He then spoke of his positive faith and confidence that God meant to bring him to life again by raising him from death, and urged upon Isaac the acceptance of that faith and confidence. He ended by pointing out that he could resist, could run away, but in doing so he would be resisting not his father but the God who gave him life. He exhorted him to do as his father had done—not wait until all meanings were clear, but to put himself in God's hands and accept the divine will as his own. Somehow God would bring good out of all this darkness and mystery. Isaac could be assured, as Abraham was, that he should in some way or other be restored, after he had been reduced to ashes, and have every divine promise fulfilled to him.

Isaac said very little to Joseph of the tumult that had filled his own soul while his father made his explanation and appeal. There was something too sacred about the great experience of his life to be talked about. He said only, "I replied to my father, 'Father, there is but one course to take for you or for me when God commands. That is the course of obedi-

18

ence. I understand now what you must do. I shall not seek to prevent you. I am in your hands—and in the hands of God.'"

Having thus gained the consent of his son, Abraham, with his breaking heart praising God that he had such a son, bound him hand and foot, and laid him upon the wood of the altar. Then, with confidence and faith unshaken, and obedience unbroken, he lifted the knife to slay the victim.

And Joseph, as the moving story unfolded and reached its climax, knew not whether to admire more the resolution of the father or the submission of the son. But there was born in him in that moment the resolution never to bring disgrace on such progenitors as God had given him. He determined that in all that should befall him, God's will should always be first, that if he could but learn that will, he would follow it, whatever consequences might come to him.

Jehovah-jireh

Isaac finished his narrative by saying that only the interposition of God Himself prevented the completion of this extraordinary sacrifice. The faith of His servant had been sufficiently tried. A voice sounded from heaven, checking the down-stroke of the uplifted knife, stopping the fatal blow. The heavenly voice said, "Abraham!"

"Yes, Lord, I am here."

"Do the lad no hurt; let him alone. I know now that thou fearest God; for my sake thou wast ready to give up thine only son."

And as Abraham looked about him, there behind him was a ram with horns entangled in the underbrush. This he took and offered as a burnt sacrifice instead of his son.

Isaac closed his thrilling story by saying that "Abraham called the name of that place Jehovah-jireh, the Lord will provide," or "the Lord will see to it."

As Joseph in the late afternoon walked to his home encampment he was in profound thought. "Jehovah-jireh, the Lord will see to it!" What a motto for a man to carry through life! What a motto to shape a life, to build a life! He would take it for his own. Could he but learn the will of God for himself, the purpose of God for his life, then he could trust all things to God as he carried out that will. All things he could leave in God's hands. With him it should be God's will, not his. Then "the Lord will see to it."

19

CHAPTER 4

Teachers and Lessons

JOSEPH'S grandfather Isaac was not his only teacher and teller of stories during the years of his boyhood. His father, Jacob, also added to the store of his knowledge. When Joseph returned home from Isaac's encampment, and the evening meal was over, he usually could get his father to relate to him the stories of his own varied experiences. He learned from Jacob of that hasty flight from his brother's wrath after Jacob had wrested the birthright from him, and the trickery practiced by his father upon his grandfather to obtain Esau's blessing as well. Jacob made no attempt to conceal from his son his own sorry character during his earlier years. But he also faithfully related the high points of his experiences in the dealings God had with him and the promises and providences that had come to him.

Thus Joseph learned the thrilling Bethel story of the staircase that reached from earth to heaven, with angels of God on it going up and down, and God standing at the top speaking great words of promise to his father. He learned, too, of the manner in which his father met his mother, of their love, of Grandfather Laban's trickery, of his father's long years of servitude, his growing family and wealth, his decision to return with his family and possessions to his old home and father, and his reconciliation with his brother Esau.

God Becoming Real

With the deepest interest he heard the account of his father's encounter with the God of Abraham and Isaac at Penuel, together with the new name and new character then bestowed. This was the most interesting and impressive of all. God had met with his father. God had changed Jacob's nature. God had led him, delivered him, blessed him, attended him, been his guide and counselor. Just as God had appeared in Abraham's life and affairs, and in Isaac's, so had He come into the life and affairs of his father, Jacob. Would God manifest Himself in his life as well?

God was becoming very real to Joseph. His thoughts were much occupied with what God had done in the history of his family, what He had meant to them, what great promises He had made to his line, what a glorious future He had spread before them. God came into human lives, made plans for individual people, commissioned them to perform His will, used them to carry out His purposes, and made them His agents in bringing to pass great enterprises and achieving important objectives.

In the inner world of Joseph's thoughts there was developing an eager, intense longing to know this God for himself. He could think of no more exhilarating life than one spent in the service of the God his fathers knew.

The stories of his father and grandfather provided Joseph with the only education he ever had. It was based on two facts, the greatest facts within the reach of human knowledge. The first and most important of all facts in Joseph's time remains the first and most important fact of our time—the fact of GOD. The force behind every thought of your brain, every beat of your heart, every breath of your body—GOD. The element in which you live and move and have your being—GOD. The final irreducible and inescapable denominator of your universe—GOD. No man's life is rightly centered and guided to a proper end if that supreme truth is missing from his knowledge. There is no other truth that compares in importance for successful living with the truth that there is a benevolent God who is working out His plans and purposes in the affairs of men.

It is not sufficient merely to know that God is. The second fact is that God reigns. That He is in control. That makes all the difference between feebleness and strength, between failure and success, between despair and assurance, for every person who will lay hold of it and make it the abiding conviction of his life.

The conviction of this second fact, strong as steel, firm as a rock, and stirring as a battle cry, was put into words by John on Patmos—words that have in them the enduring granite of the ages, "The Lord God omnipotent reigneth" (Rev. 19:6).

21

It was in the light of this conviction that Joseph grew to manhood and was able to meet and conquer all that life brought to him.

The Fact of God's Will

Alongside the supreme affirmation that God is, and sees, and knows, and cares, and guides—upon which Joseph built his life—I would lay down another basic fact, or truth, that influenced his whole life. That is *the will of God.* God not only exists, He also has a will. That will has reference to all things taking place in the world—all persons, all events, all history. That will has reference to you; it is willing something relating to you, now and every moment you breathe. By consulting that will we learn how to live, how to move, when to act, what to do, what to say. Everything we do and say, every move we make, every choice of our daily experience, every decision at which we arrive, is either in harmony with the will of God or contrary to it.

Moment by moment, day and night, hour after hour, every person is either in or out of harmony with the will of God. That will pervades the universe. There never can be a moment when it would be true to say, "God has no particular desire, no definite purpose, for me just now. This moment I can do as I please, without reference to Him and His plan for me." That is never true.

Joseph had slowly come to understand and believe that there was no more important life he could live, no greater achievement to strive for, than that in which he could obtain a knowledge of God's will for the purpose of putting his own life in line with it and carrying it out in all he did. If God truly had a will regarding himself and his affairs and his future and what he was to do with his life, he desired above all things to know what that will was, what God's plan for his life was, what God purposed Joseph should do for Him in carrying out His great purposes on earth.

The Secret of Successful Living

The secret of successful living is very simple, very plain; so plain, indeed, as to be wholly within the understanding of a child. It is just to do God's will, to be in tune with the Infinite. It is this secret, which Joseph learned in early life, that made his later life the saga of success it became. I know of nothing more comforting, more energizing, more inspiring than the conviction that God is thinking of me and thinking for me; that He has a plan for my life and a purpose to be accomplished by my living.

It was this conviction that came into Joseph's heart as a result of the moving stories of his father and grandfather. It was this conviction that prompted Paul to exclaim at the first moment of his conversion, "Lord, what wilt thou have me to do?" It was because of this conviction in David's heart that God described him as "a man after mine own heart, which shall fulfil all my will."

The true plan of the ideal Christian life is set forth in these words of Scripture. What is it? We must have a definition, that we may know it. We must have a description, that we may follow it.

Here is the definition: "A man after mine own heart." Here is the description of how to live it: "Which shall fulfil all my will."

The sweet general truth of these words is simply this: The supreme end of life is to do God's will.

We do not come to push our way, to seek success, to make a name for ourselves, to accomplish great tasks, to go to distant lands, to perform herculean feats. David described Christ's aim in life: "I come to do thy will, O God." The Saviour confirmed this when He said, "I seek not mine own will, but the will of the Father which hath sent me" (John 5:30).

A God-sent Man

"He sent a man before them, even Joseph, who was sold for a servant: whose feet they hurt with fetters: he was laid in iron: until the time that his word came: the word of the Lord tried him" (Psalm 105:17-19).

This text says that he was God's man. "He [God] sent a man before them, even Joseph." That means he was God's man. He was God-sent—to do a specific, designated task. He was sent before his family; he was sent before his nation, because God had in mind to do something with that nation, and this seventeen-year-old boy was God's agent in the accomplishment of it.

God Has a Plan for Your Life

Joseph possessed an implicit and profound belief, which no developments seemed to shake or alter, that God had a definite, positive plan for his life; that there was something in the mind of God for him to accomplish, some purpose for him to fulfill, some program, divinely made, to carry out.

23

He was conscious always, in all circumstances, that he was under the discipline of God, under the tuition of the Divine Spirit, and he surrendered himself to that Spirit to be directed at every step and in every decision of life. He looked upon himself as a man under orders, divine orders, as God's man, God's agent, to hold himself always at God's command.

One of the purposes of this book is to emphasize that whoever accepts the teaching of the Bible that God has a plan for his life, and keeps that fact before him always, is bound to see his most cherished dreams fulfilled and the will of God for him completely realized. Such a person will recognize in circumstances only the tools that God uses to shape and mold and fit him for his destiny, will yield himself to the impressions and convictions that come from above, and permit them to take him outside the developments that are immediately around him and which touch him. He will yield himself willingly and happily and agreeably and devotedly to such influences.

We Live in God's Thoughts

It is a great comfort to believe that you live in God's thoughts, that He is planning for you in love, that He is shaping your life, that He has assigned you something to accomplish for Him, that you are His agent to fulfill His purpose, and that He will control for good every circumstance that is permitted to touch you. Yes, that knowledge is a great comfort. Moreover, that knowledge is worthy of our confidence. And still more, it is just as true of you as it was of Joseph.

Let a man believe that, and apply it to every circumstance of life, and it will result in the cultivation of his spiritual nature, the culture and development of his spiritual mind. There will come to that man great thoughts and a wide-open understanding of God's purposes, a far-reaching vision and timely adjustment to sudden setbacks and sudden promotions. That man will go steadily, inexorably forward in the way God has marked out for him to take, and to the places for which God has prepared him.

No Accidents in Such a Life

No accident can happen to such a man. Things do not happen to him by chance. He is God's man, God's agent, and everything that occurs to him comes to him through the hand of God.

24

Nothing can really hurt such a man. His feelings can be hurt, he can be plunged into terrible grief, he can be shocked by the hatred of brethren; but these things work together to his real good as he believes God and yields to His disciplining hand.

The greatest fact in the universe is the existence of God. God is. Each individual is dealing with an invisible Person who controls the universe and has a plan for his life.

The second greatest fact of the universe is the will of God. God has a will and all things are under control of that will. That will has marked out a plan for my life.

Just to believe these two facts equips a man to live, equips him for success, equips him for achievement, equips him to accomplish the will of God. Get everything else you can, but with all your getting do not fail to get these fundamental truths.

Joseph believed God; he knew God; he loved God; he followed God; he trusted God. That was Joseph's essential preparation for life, the sum total of his education. It was quite enough.

An education without God is an incomplete and inadequate education, even for this life. Just to know God and believe Him, to love Him and to follow Him, is adequate for success similar to Joseph's.

I invite you to develop, by the grace of the Lord, a rock-bound faith in God Himself, to take Him as your counsel, to look upon Him as your friend, to believe that He has a plan and purpose for you to fulfill, confidently to expect Him to bring you at last into that place of service and final happiness that will identify you with His people through the ages to come.

CHAPTER 5

The Forward Look

I T IS a great thing for any youth to discover what he is fit for, what his life is to be, what he is in the world to accomplish, and to acquire a sense of mission. If, in addition to his own groping impressions about it, he is fortunate enough to have come to him the realization that what he is to do with his life is what God has appointed for him, and is fitting him to do, he is doubly blessed. He can then settle down to his work with a comforting sense of solid assurance, and patiently carry on each day, awaiting God's time for the accomplishment of God's purposes and designs.

Such a discovery saves a man much fretting and disappointment and waste of time—to come early in life to an understanding of what he is to do, what it is he is fitted to accomplish, and exactly what work he is to be about. If he can so analyze his personal gifts and station in life—see with unclouded vision the circumstances, the conditions, and the complications that belong to and surround him in his associations and relations to others, or to the world—and learn to discern the will of God as it teaches him what he is and for what he ought to live, he will indeed have taken a great step forward.

A Fixed Course

More and more Joseph's thoughts centered in his own future. He was endowed with a remarkable intelligence. There had been a deep response in his inmost being to the great stories of God's dealings with Abraham, Isaac, and Jacob, related to him during many months by his father and grandfather. He possessed a susceptible heart, and it had been attracted irresistibly to the great God of his people. He had reached a decision which he continued to maintain as long as life lasted. That decision could well be expressed in the words "This God is our God for ever and ever: he will be our guide even unto death."

Among his brothers he was alone in this decision. They had little sympathy for him. And the developments that the passing days brought to him, the experiences through which he passed, served to drive him more apart, and tended to cause him to strike his roots deeper on the side of God.

Home Life Not Ideal

The home life of Joseph was far from ideal, and at times it must have been most unpleasant and hard to bear. Not in the modern sense but nevertheless in a very real sense, he lived in a divided home. In the encampment of Jacob four divisions existed. They did not, it is true, form separate households. It might have been better if they had, so far as the maintenance of harmony was concerned.

These divisions were composed of Leah and her sons, Zilpah and her sons, Bilhah and her sons, and the sons of Rachel. Even a superficial reading of the Bible narrative is sufficient to disclose that Joseph's ten half-brothers had no scruples against riding roughshod over the feelings and wishes of Joseph or anyone else who seemed in any degree to stand in their way.

This disposition of his brothers, as well as his own motherless condition, together with the standards, principles, and ideals he had obtained from the recitals by his father and grandfather of the history of God's dealings with his family, would naturally have a pronounced tendency to increase Joseph's loneliness and his concern for his brothers.

Moreover, Jacob was unwise, not for having a preference for Joseph above all his children but for manifesting it openly for all to see. Jacob should have learned better from his own experience. He had suffered from a similar favoritism of his own father for Esau, and no good had come out of his mother's preference for him above Esau. However, the folly of his own parents taught him nothing, and he repeated that folly himself in his own family.

The record is that "Israel loved Joseph more than all his children." This is quite understandable and not to be wondered at. Joseph was endowed, according to rabbinical lore, with a knowledge beyond his years. He was the first-born son of the only woman Jacob had truly loved. He

27

had a natural sweetness of disposition and lovableness of character, and he most tenderly loved and waited on his father.

That Princely Coat

It was because of this doting fondness and preference for Jacob's favorite son that Joseph was distinguished above the rest by his father's gift of "the coat of many colours." It may be that we have been accustomed to think of this garment as a sort of patchwork blazer and have wondered that grown men allowed themselves to be whipped into a passion by the sight of it. But there is more to it than that.

Another version has it that his father "dressed him in a coat that was all embroidery." It was such a robe as was worn only by the opulent and the noble, by kings' sons, and particularly by those who had no need to toil for their living. In short, it was the garment of a prince. It was given to Joseph for the purpose of marking his superiority, of making a distinction between him and his more rude brothers. No wonder they bore a grudge against him!

When Jacob gave such a robe to Joseph it meant but one thing to them, and they could think of nothing else. It did not excite their ridicule as might have been expected. It aroused their envy, their jealousy, their deep hatred. In those days the father's will was law. When, therefore, they saw Joseph set apart from them by this robe of state, this truly princely garment, they understood that their father, in effect, was declaring that this younger son was to have the rich inheritance, the birthright, and was designated for headship, while they must be content with their lives of toil. Little wonder that the record is, "And when his brethren saw that their father loved him more than all his brethren, they hated him, and could not speak peaceably unto him."

This hatred was aggravated by his frankness, his plain speaking. He "brought unto his father their evil report." Some have understood this to mean that Joseph was a petty talebearer, going out of his way to poison his father against his brothers. This, however, was not at all the case, and puts Joseph out of character altogether as designing to get his brothers in trouble. That view cannot be accepted. Many Biblical scholars believe history indicates that Joseph had been set over the sons of Zilpah and the sons of Bilhah in their occupation as shepherds, and was consequently responsible to their father, as overseer, to report to him the welfare of the flocks and to give a faithful account of the manner in which each of his brothers performed his duties.

His Faithfulness Accounted Talebearing

Consequently, the "evil report" that Joseph brought to their father, so far from indicating that he was a talebearer, seeking to bring his brothers into trouble, discloses rather that there were circumstances not only justifying but even demanding the exposure of the evil conduct of these men. It was foolish for his father to place Joseph in a post of superintendency, but being in that place made Joseph responsible to their father for an account of their behavior. And as he was jealous for the family name, which according to the record, they had already made "to stink among the inhabitants of the land," he believed he should not conceal their evil conduct, their neglect of duty, their delinquencies, but let his father know just how matters stood. This he did; and it greatly enraged his brothers.

It is always so. You may have experienced something similar. You will if you live by principle. The evil always hate the good. "Every one that doeth evil hateth the light." It is the way of the world.

We may well be uneasy if the world about us, the company with which we travel, loves us and speaks well of us. We are in danger then. We are as followers of the Lord to be salt, which is characteristically pure and stinging, in the midst of the world's corruptions. When our lives develop a pronounced contrast to the world they constitute a reproof, and that reproof arouses virulent hate.

This may have been, may still be, your experience. If it should be, then follow Joseph's example. Go on doing right. Do not allow yourself to develop self-pity, to be thrown into depression. Your experience is no different from that of the Lord you serve. He suffered the same treatment from His own. Nevertheless, when He was reviled, He reviled not again. He did not answer back or threaten. He committed Himself to God, who judgeth righteously. So your time will come at last, and God shall vindicate you and exchange your sorrows for joys. "Trust in the Lord, and do good. . . . Fret not thyself in any wise to do evil. For evildoers shall be cut off: but those that wait upon the Lord, they shall inherit the earth." "He shall bring forth thy righteousness as the light, and thy judgment as the noonday."

CHAPTER 6

Meaningful Dreams

FROM dwelling upon the past, Joseph had come to think more and more upon the future. One of the chief things that sent his thoughts in that direction was found in his impressive dreams. Moreover, his dreams were the cause of a deepening hatred by his half brothers.

"Joseph dreamed a dream, and he told it his brethren: and they hated him yet the more" (Gen. 37:5).

With the naïveté and innocence of his years, and without realizing the hatred his brothers already had for him, and with no awareness of the effect the telling of his dream would have upon them, Joseph proceeded to relate what his dream had been.

He and his brothers were, he said, together at work in the field, binding sheaves. All at once the sheaf he was binding rose and stood upright, at which the sheaves of his brothers gathered around his sheaf and "made obeisance to my sheaf."

The significance of this was not lost upon his brothers. They broke into indignation and scorn. Their words were "Shalt thou indeed reign over us? or shalt thou indeed have dominion over us?"

Nor did it end there. "He dreamed yet another dream, and told it his brethren." This time "the sun and the moon and the eleven stars made obeisance" to him. Even his father felt this was going too far. He chided Joseph by saying, "What is this dream that thou hast dreamed? Shall I and thy mother and thy brethren indeed come to bow down ourselves to thee to the earth?"

Nevertheless, his father, though he was moved to publicly rebuke Joseph, was impressed with the obvious meaning of the dream. The record is that "his father observed the saying." He could not help wondering what the Lord had in mind for his beloved son.

MEANINGFUL DREAMS

Destined to High Honor

By these dreams God pointed out to Joseph that he was destined to high honor. A day would come when all his family should make obeisance to him.

It has been said that Joseph was unwise and indiscreet to divulge all this to his brothers, as he should have realized the effect it was bound to have on them in deepening their envy and hatred. Very likely that is true, but even this absence of tact was evidently a part of the divine plan. Without a deep and blazing hatred they would have been without an adequate incentive to take the steps that put Joseph in Egypt; and God's later plans made it wholly necessary for Joseph to go to Egypt. Their envy and hatred blinded these men to every consideration but that of getting rid of this conceited dreamer whose dreams were so distasteful to them. From that time forward their thoughts kept swinging in the direction of discovering some method of getting rid of their troublesome brother, and thus preventing his dreams from coming true.

Joseph's dreams were bound to drive his thoughts in upon himself and out upon his future. He possessed a quick intelligence. He could but understand that God had destined him to accomplish some important mission that would result in high honor. He must have become aware of his own developing powers. He could not be indifferent to his own destiny. The very attitude of his brothers toward him, as well as that of his father, must have made him self-conscious and introspective. Evidently they felt that these dreams meant something of great importance. He felt the same. His father obviously considered there was something superior about him. Hence the princely garment that so angered his brothers. This garment along with his dreams was intolerably exasperating to them. They were coarse and unscrupulous men, and the sense they had of Joseph's superiority rankled within them. They could scarcely wait for the time when opportunity would make it possible for them to do something about it. So they cherished their grudge while Joseph cherished his dreams.

The great adventures of this lad's life were about to begin. He did not know—he could not know—what they were to be. But God had been getting him ready for them. God had in mind one of the most important developments of human history, and this lad was to be His agent in bringing it about.

31

Human history both past and future is all open before the eyes of the Divine Sovereign of the world. He plans world affairs a long time in advance, and He chooses His agents carefully. His plans and purposes for the long future made it necessary that the family of Israel should migrate into Egypt. And through Joseph He was initiating the developments that would bring about the migration.

That migration from Canaan into Egypt was one of the main events in the history of God's dealings with men and the carrying out of His agelong purpose of human salvation. It was surrounded with enormous difficulties and required extraordinary means to bring it about. Even the preparatory steps required about twenty years.

This removal of Israel from Canaan to Egypt was no new or hasty plan of God. It had been long contemplated. Abraham had been made aware of it. God had said to him, "Know of a surety that thy seed shall be a stranger in a land that is not their's, and shall serve them; and they shall afflict them four hundred years; and also that nation, whom they shall serve, will I judge: and afterward shall they come out with great substance" (Gen. 15:13, 14).

The reasons why God planned to take the children of Israel out of Canaan and place them in Egypt are numerous. Some of them are quite apparent. The chief one among them was stated by God when He endeavored to reassure Jacob at the time the migration was becoming a matter of actual experience. "Fear not," He said to the old man who was fearful and uncertain about abandoning the Land of Promise to go into a strange country. "Fear not to go down into Egypt; I will there make of thee a great nation."

God's Plans

This purpose of God for Israel could not be realized in Canaan. The difficulties were too great. So the far-reaching purposes of God for His people made necessary their removal from Canaan. Canaan was rude and semibarbarous. For more than two centuries Abraham and his descendants had been shifting about in it as pilgrims and roving nomads. No evidence had yet developed that God's promise that this land was to be theirs was being fulfilled. That promise had been of a land and of a seed. This land was plainly not theirs. And Abraham's seed, so far from being innumerable as the sand of the sea and the uncountable stars of heaven, numbered only two score or three score persons. One encampment was sufficient to contain them all. The great increase in numbers that was part of the divine promise had not developed.

So long as they remained small there would be little likelihood of trouble in Canaan. Just in proportion as they increased in number, the hostility of the surrounding tribes would also increase. Their very size would kindle the suspicion and arouse the jealousy and hatred of their neighbors, who would be quick to resent the developing pressure against them of a growing people with peculiar forms of worship, alien customs, and a different God. Collision between themselves and the tribes about them would then become unavoidable, particularly as it became known what their real character and pretensions and expectations were. It could not be long hidden that they looked forward to taking over the land of Canaan for themselves and becoming masters.

In such a collision between a few score nomads, whose ambitions and purposes impelled them to seek supremacy, and the peoples about them, who would have to be suppressed if such ambitions were realized, the result would be war for their extermination.

It was to avoid such perils, as well as to assure the growth of Israel into nationhood without such contingencies, that God would remove the household of Jacob from Canaan to a land where they could have both protection and seclusion. In the land of Goshen they would be secure from molestation, both by royal protection and by the caste prejudices of the Egyptians, who hated all foreigners, and shepherds in particular. They could there achieve such prosperity and attain so rapidly the magnitude of a nation that they would be able, when God's time came, to return to Canaan and under the leadership of God bring about the fulfillment of the divine promises relating to the land of Canaan. In Goshen they would acquire every advantage for bringing about the transition from a family to a nation.

Israel to Go to Egypt

It was therefore the divine purpose for Jacob and his family to go into Egypt. Joseph's dreams, the princely garment, the jealousy, malice, and envy of his brothers, were all a part of the arrangements by which that migration would be made possible.

The stay of Israel in Egypt would serve another purpose of major importance. It would bring the growing family into connection with the most civilized people of ancient times, and thus aid them to outgrow their own semibarbarity. They were shepherds and did not possess, so far as we know, even the basic arts of civilization. They had only most rudimentary ideas of law and justice. There was little to hold them together and produce the form and strength of solidarity other than the tenuous expectation that God designed them for leadership and eminence.

In Egypt they would come under the influences of a land where government had been so long established and law was so thoroughly administered that life and property had become safe, where science was making great strides, where all the arts were in familiar use. It was a school that the enlarging family of Israel greatly needed; no more suitable discipline and training could be obtained to shape them, and give them room to grow, so that they might be made ready for the fulfillment of God's purposes for them.

And so it was a part of God's design that the family of Israel should go down to Egypt.

We must not overlook another reason why the children of Israel must be gotten away from Canaan. They were to be a separate people, separate from the world. They were to be God's people, to receive God's law and God's Word. From them were to come teachers, singers, poets, prophets. From them also was to come the Messiah, the world's Redeemer, and His redemptive religion. Therefore they must be a holy people, a peculiar people, a people of unmixed blood. In Canaan that could not be. The surrounding tribes would mingle with them, demand their daughters for their sons, and win the sons of Jacob for their daughters.

In Goshen they would have a place in which they would be shielded against all this. There the temptation to intermarry would not exist. The Egyptians were proud and exclusive. They would have no association with foreigners, most especially shepherds. The family of Jacob would be insulated, most effectively shut off by themselves. They had no choice in Goshen but to grow up together, separate from all other people.

God's plan, therefore, was that the family should be moved out of Canaan and into Egypt, indeed into the seclusiveness and insularity of Goshen.

How was this to be done? This boy Joseph, seventeen years of age, was chosen as God's agent to bring it about. He did not know it. We seldom ever know when God is using us to bring about divine objectives. And we do not need to. We need only see to it that our lives are given up to do His known will, that we are walking in His known ways. Then we may be confidently assured that we are being used to accomplish divine purposes.

While Joseph did not dream of the magnitude of God's purposes that he was to be instrumental in bringing about, his dreams had given him some idea of great future developments in which he was to play an important part. He gained an impression, vague indeed, but nevertheless quite definite enough to make him contemplative, that he was chosen by God to become a blessing to others, to his family, and he was to be so far advanced above his brothers that they would look up to him and pay him homage as if he were in rulership over them.

There is no evidence that such a revelation and such a recognition produced in him any thought of self-exaltation. Rather, it is clear that the effect was the conviction that his higher powers were to be used for the benefit of his brothers. The high destiny that the dreams revealed to be his was to come to him for doing service so important that his family would honor him for it. The superior talents and opportunities given him were to be used not for himself, but that they might benefit others.

If we could all catch such a vision—that our natural talents and gifts as well as our acquired abilities and attainments were given to us for others, and that we are stewards of them—it is likely that we would find ourselves more fully and definitely used by the Divine Spirit to accomplish God's purposes.

Joseph had no knowledge and no thought of the path over which God was to take him in reaching the high dignity of his foreshadowing dreams. It would not be long, however, before he would realize that the path marked out for him was neither easy nor short. The first step in that path was now about to be taken.

CHAPTER 7

Sold as a Slave

MEN who cherish hatred are quick to see and seize upon opportunities to visit their malice upon the objects of their detesta-
tion. It was not long until such an opportunity came to Joseph's half
brothers, and quite unexpectedly to them.

The encampment of Jacob at Hebron was a vast one, and the rich
pasture lands spread widely on all sides. Extensive as these were, however, they proved insufficient for the enormous flocks of the patriarch and
his sons. Jacob's wealth in flocks and herds was very great. It became
necessary, therefore, at times for the brothers to seek pasture farther afield.
This meant an extensive migration of sheep and cattle in search of adequate pasturage.

Shortly after the occasion of Joseph's dreams, and while his brothers
were still inflamed with hatred of him, it became necessary for them to
take their flocks away from the headquarters encampment at Hebron
in their search for pasture. As they talked this over with their father,
their thoughts turned to the lush pasture lands of Shechem, fifty miles to
the north. They knew that country, for Jacob had settled there at first on
his return to Canaan from Padan-aram. It was there that the sons of
Jacob had grievously wronged the people of Shechem in connection
with the affair of their sister Dinah. They had not ventured to go near it
since, for fear that the inhabitants would resent their coming and drive
them away.

Nothing would do on this occasion, however, but that they should
seek pasture at Shechem, regardless of the risk. So they made the venture,
braving the anger of the Shechemites, and drove their flocks and herds
by easy stages to this rich pasture. About what happened, the record is
silent, but something occurred, we know, that made them depart from

Shechem with their whole entourage and seek pasture fifteen miles farther north at Dothan.

Jacob's Growing Anxiety

As the days passed at the home camp, bringing no word from his sons, the uneasiness of Jacob increased. Evidently some weeks had dragged slowly by since he had received any tidings of their welfare. The memory of the past produced a growing anxiety in the father's mind. And this grew so overpoweringly that it led him to do what under normal circumstances he would not have thought of doing. He decided to send Joseph to Shechem.

The two sons of Rachel, Joseph and Benjamin, had remained with their father at Hebron. Loving them with the same deep devotion he had felt for their mother, he had kept them with him. Now, however, his alarm growing for his absent sons and the flocks, and after much hesitation, he determined to send Joseph to find them and bring him word of their safety. He called Joseph and said, "Do not thy brethren feed the flock in Shechem? come, and I will send thee unto them."

Joseph's response was "Here am I."

There was no hesitation on Joseph's part. Just as quickly as he knew his father's will he expressed his willingness to obey it. This was not because he was in ignorance of the dangers that confronted him. He knew he was going into real peril. Not only were there perils of streams to cross, of robbers, of wild beasts, of lonely nights, but there was the animosity of his brothers. He was quite aware of their hatred. His father wanted him to go. That was enough. He went. Not alone because it was his father's wish but because he loved his brothers, notwithstanding their hatred.

It could not have been easy for the aging father to send his favorite son on this mission. Nevertheless, he loaded him with delicacies for the brothers and sent him off to find them and bring him word again. He did not dream that more than twenty years would pass before he saw this dear lad again. Do we ever know, even at the most casual partings, that we shall see our loved ones again? They pass out of sight around the corner of a street, or on a train, and are gone. Is it for hours? Or for days? Or for years? Or forever? None of us know.

Joseph finally arrived at Shechem. He met with deep disappointment.

His brothers were not there. A man came upon him wandering in a field, and on learning the object of his search, informed him that his brothers had been there but had gone to Dothan. So Joseph started on for Dothan.

His Brothers' Hatred

His brothers saw him coming across the fields in their direction. They saw him, the record declares, "afar off, even before he came near unto them." What they saw first was that princely coat, embroidered all over. And their hatred flamed afresh. "They conspired against him." To one another they said, "Look, this is our chance. This dreamer is putting himself in our power. Come now, therefore, and let us put him to death and throw his carcass in one of the pits hereabouts. We will report that some wild beast has destroyed him. Then we will see what will become of his dreams."

The first thing they did was to strip him of that ornate coat, the badge of his favoritism and superiority. It is likely that they handled him roughly as they relieved him of the hated garment.

Doubtless he would have been slain at once and his body flung into a pit had it not been for the eldest brother's merciful pleading for him. Reuben, with the purpose in mind of later delivering him from them altogether, said, "No, no, men, let us not get the guilt of blood upon us. After all, he is our brother. The pit, yes; but alive, not dead."

It should not be overlooked that this was more than generous from Reuben, the one "unstable as water." For Reuben as the first-born of Jacob's sons had a greater claim to the birthright than the others. He had been deprived of the birthright as a result of his grievous and revolting sin with Bilhah, his father's wife. It might have been expected, therefore, that his hatred for Joseph, who was believed to have been put into his place, would have exceeded that of the others. His better nature, however, broke through at times, and this was one of the times. He was a creature of impulse. His impulse now was to save Joseph from the malice of his brothers, get him into a pit to save him from being slain out of hand, and later draw him up and restore him to his father.

The brothers fell in with his proposal. Joseph would be effectually disposed of in any case. They were not unwilling to murder their brother if that was necessary to rid themselves of this troublesome dreamer and upstart. But letting him come to his death by starving was better than murder, at least for them. So they lowered Joseph into one of the numerous cisterns that were common in Canaan, and which, as in the case of Jeremiah, were sometimes used to hold prisoners. An explorer in that land, Lieutenant Anderson, of the Palestine Exploration Enterprise, writes regarding these pits:

"The numerous rock-hewn cisterns that are found everywhere would furnish a suitable pit in which they might have thrust him; and as these cisterns are shaped like a bottle, with a narrow mouth, it would be impossible for anyone imprisoned within it to extricate himself without assistance."—*The Land and the Book: Central Palestine and Phoenicia*, p. 168.

Joseph's Thoughts

More than once I have allowed my mind to contemplate what the thoughts and feelings of this seventeen-year-old lad must have been as these men, his own father's sons, lowered him into the pit. These were his brothers, men with whom he had lived all his life. He had had two remarkable dreams about them, dreams that he believed were given him of God. These dreams made plain that a time would come when he would have supremacy over his brothers, and they would make obeisance to him. And now these very men had seized him and put him into a pit as their prisoner. This was a far distance from anything he had expected.

In the narrative itself at this point there is no word to inform us what Joseph's thoughts were. Long afterward, however, there is a glimpse given us of the heartbreak he experienced. When his brothers were in Egypt seeking grain to sustain their families, their guilty consciences reminded them of their heartlessness to their brother, and they said one to another, "We are verily guilty concerning our brother, in that we saw the anguish of his soul, when he besought us, and we would not hear" (Gen. 42:21).

"He *besought* us." That is a revealing word. When they proposed putting him to death, he besought them. What a spectacle it brings up! This lad, in the rough hands of men determined to take his life, with all his heart in his face and voice, he besought them. And then when they forced him to descend into that dark, dreary, and dank prison house of a pit, as perhaps a vision of his father flashed into his mind, and the prospect

39

confronted him of perishing alone there in the darkness, the tears began to flow, and he besought them. And they would not hear. It is not difficult to bring the scene before us.

Extreme Cruelty

His brothers turned away, "and they sat down to eat bread." Regaling themselves on the very delicacies Joseph had brought from their father, they had no concern for their brother whom they had left to die! It was an exhibition of extreme cruelty and callousness. And ever after they were unable to dismiss it from their minds. It remained with them and plagued them through the years that followed. They fell into the habit of attributing everything that went wrong with them and their affairs as retribution upon them for the terrible wrong they had done.

Meanwhile, Joseph became quiet and calm in his gloomy prison. It came to him that he was in no greater extremity than his grandfather Isaac had been that day on Mount Moriah when God sent him deliverance. Nor was he in greater straits than his dear father had been as he waited to meet with Esau. He reminded himself that in both cases the God of his fathers had provided a way of escape. And he was greatly cheered. He recalled his dreams and their assurance of future service for his family and his own destiny. And he brought to mind what his great ancestor Abraham had named Moriah when God had provided deliverance for Isaac. "Jehovah-jireh," "the Lord will provide" or "the Lord will see to it." Comfort flowed into his desolate heart. The God who had cared for his fathers would care for him. Some way of deliverance would come. His anguish of heart subsided. He recalled that he had determined to take as his life motto "Jehovah-jireh: The Lord will see to it." He would look to the Lord to "see to it."

Nor did he look in vain. The Lord was seeing to it. Reuben, after seeing his suggestion of putting him into a pit carried out, went off somewhere, planning to return at a time when the others would be absent, and draw Joseph from the pit and restore him to his father.

God Had Other Plans

But it did not work out that way. God had other plans. He had used Reuben to save Joseph from immediate destruction. Now He arranged to take Joseph out of their hands completely, and send him on his way to the ultimate fulfillment of his dreams, and the realization of his great destiny.

We would not leave this particular phase of Joseph's history, however, without recognizing that in carrying out His purposes the Sovereign of the world is not thwarted by the malice, the hatreds, the cruelty, the deadly enmity, and the determined intentions and activities of bad men. Indeed, so far from these things overturning the divine plans, the God of heaven actually finds ways to use evil motives and purposes to bring about His own designs. "In everything God works for good with those who love him." God worked for good with Joseph on this occasion, and on all other occasions of his life.

While the brothers with heartless indifference "sat down to eat," and Reuben had gone on some errand, a caravan of merchants journeyed along on their way to Egypt to dispose of their wares. Their route took them past Dothan. Judah looked up from his meal and saw them approaching; he recognized instantly who and what they were. There leaped into his mind at once an idea for solving the problem of the disposal of Joseph that seemed far superior to that of letting him starve to death in the pit. At the same time it presented the opportunity of making a monetary profit out of the occasion.

He turned to his brothers and said, "What profit is it if we slay our brother, and conceal his blood? Come, and let us sell him to the Ishmeelites, and let not our hand be upon him; for he is our brother and our flesh."

Ah, that was a brighter idea than Reuben's. Moreover, it held a prospect of personal gain. Consequently, the brothers seized upon it at once. Selling Joseph seemed so much better than slaying Joseph, so much milder, that they could actually argue that it was practically a virtue in contrast with fratricide. It made them feel almost good to be able to take care of the unpleasant matter so pleasantly.

So "they drew and lifted up Joseph out of the pit, and sold Joseph to the Ishmeelites for twenty pieces of silver." And dividing the money among them, they considered that they had done a good stroke of business and that they had disposed once and forever of this troublesome brother of theirs, and most effectively prevented his exasperating dreams from ever being fulfilled. They did not, and they could not, of course, realize that so far from preventing the fulfillment of his dreams they had taken a most important step to bring about their full realization.

41

And now, having as they thought permanently disposed of Joseph, the brothers found it necessary to account to their father for what they had done. There were a lot of things to think through; there was a story to concoct; there were explanations to be made. There was a case to be made out, and case-making is not always easy, particularly when it is designed to deceive. Reuben had returned by this time, and was so grievously disappointed to discover that his well-laid plot had come to nothing and Joseph was gone that he rent his clothes in the violence of his grief. But as always in the case of Reuben, this mood quickly changed and he joined his brothers in inventing an account of Joseph's disappearance that would hide the truth from their father. They must all say the same thing; no discrepancies must be allowed to creep into their account.

Their Lying Report

In formulating their lying report they found they could make good use of the hated coat of many colors. They killed a goat, caught its blood in a basin, dipped the exasperating garment in the blood, brought it to their father, and with an appearance of innocent perplexity said:

"Look, we found this in the field. We cannot be sure, but we felt you should examine it to determine whether it can be the coat which belonged to Joseph."

The effect was terrible. Sorrow settled down on the patriarch. He knew the coat. It was indeed Joseph's. The story of his sons appeared to be fully confirmed. He cried out, "Joseph is without doubt rent in pieces." All their pretense of comforting him was in vain. He refused to be comforted. The light of his life was extinguished.

Meanwhile, as he mourned for Joseph as dead, his dearly loved son was in a caravan on his way to Egypt.

CHAPTER 8

From Canaan to Egypt

JOSEPH'S secondary education had begun. With the murderous
hatred of his brothers that put him into the pit, and his resulting sale
into slavery, he had matriculated into the course of training that would
give him the direct preparation for the great career of usefulness that
would fulfill his dreams and constitute his lifework. It was no easy training
upon which he was now entering. It certainly was not of his own choosing.
But the lessons he was required to learn, while extremely difficult, were
wholly necessary for the later work that he was to accomplish.

Moreover, his earlier education, what may be called his primary or
elementary course, the basic, foundation principles that he had learned
under the tutelage of Isaac and Jacob, had provided an adequate preparation for the comprehension of the much more difficult lessons he had now
to learn. The earlier lessons came crowding back into his thoughts
as he faced the new and terrifying developments that were rapidly unfolding, and they served to hold him steady and confident through the
passing days.

Chained to other slaves to prevent escape, he was now a part of the
caravan of Ishmaelites. As the caravan continued on its leisurely way to
the great market of Egypt it traveled southward from Dothan. In two or
three days, as it kept to the customary caravan route, it came close to
Hebron, where were the encampments of Jacob and Isaac, from which
Joseph had started out on his visit to the brothers but a little while before.
Joseph knew that just a little to the east, over that low ridge of hills on
their left, was home, with all its security. There, too, only such a little way
off, were father and grandfather. If he could only get word to them, how
quickly things would change for him, how speedily would he be rescued.

Over there, such a little way, his father was awaiting his return from the search he had made for his brothers. Over there was awaiting him a warm welcome and all the dear things of home and love. He was so near. Would deliverance come? He looked yearningly and eagerly at the hills that interposed between him and the black goatskin tents he knew so well.

No Deliverance Came

But no deliverance came. The men, the camels, the slaves, plodded slowly on toward Egypt, toward the cruel slavery into which his brothers had sold him, toward the unknown future; and the familiar hills slowly receded from the sight of Joseph's tear-dimmed eyes. And with them the distance lengthened with every step onward from his father, from his home, from all he had known and loved, and he entered upon a new life, a frightening new life as well as an entirely new world. What would it hold for him? He endeavored to project his mind into the future, but it was not good. The future was all a blank, dark and meaningless. He turned away from it and directed his thoughts into the past, occupying himself with the things he knew, the lessons he had learned from father and grandfather.

The great Jehovah had brought his great-grandfather into this land, had nurtured, guided, preserved him in it. He had also made him most wonderful promises of a great and magnificent future, both for himself and his posterity. His posterity was to be enormously enlarged so that it should be like the sands of the sea and as innumerable as the stars of heaven.

His grandfather Isaac too had received similar promises from Jehovah. He too had been given a significant deliverance from death in order to fulfill the promise to Abraham that "in Isaac shall thy seed be called."

His father, Jacob, had also been the recipient of these cherished promises. He had seen into heaven, had witnessed the angels going up and down on the shining staircase that linked earth with heaven. He had been told in the most solemn way that God would be with him wherever he went, and would bless him until the promises were fulfilled. God had blessed his father with great wealth, had wrought for him a wonderful deliverance from Uncle Esau, had come to him in that night at Penuel and given him another heart and another nature.

FROM CANAAN TO EGYPT

What Would Slavery Mean?

There could be no doubt that God had chosen his family, his line, and made them His own people, and that He had plans for their future that meant enlargement and greatness. Joseph believed that with all his heart. He had the most complete confidence in the God of his fathers. Moreover, there were his own dreams. They came from God, he was certain. They meant something. It was the purpose of God to do something of great service to His people through Joseph. That had been made clear. What then could his present situation—the circumstances surrounding him, the cruelty of his brothers, his passage into Egypt, his slavery—mean? How could all this have any place in the plans of God for him and his family? He was being torn away from his family. He was going to Egypt.

Egypt! The word aroused him to a sense that he had heard something about Egypt that had to do with his people. He searched his memory, and suddenly he recalled that his grandfather Isaac had told him that Jehovah had said to Abraham:

"Know of a surety that thy seed shall be a stranger in a land that is not their's, and shall serve them; and they shall afflict them four hundred years; and also that nation, whom they shall serve, will I judge: and afterward shall they come out with great substance" (Gen. 15:13, 14). Isaac had said that Abraham had believed this nation, where they were to be strangers and whom they were to serve, was Egypt. And now he, Joseph, was on his way to Egypt! And he was on his way to serve! Did it all have to do with plans that Jehovah was working out? He began to believe that it did. And he was enormously cheered by the thought.

The dear hills of home were growing dim in the distance as they went on their way. He looked back at them more than once until they disappeared altogether. There would be no rescue. His father did not know he was so near. But somehow he felt better. The deep turbulence of thought, the frightened shock that he had felt as he was lowered into the pit after looking into the blazing, murderous eyes of his brothers, had given place to an assurance that he was in the hands of the mighty God of his fathers, who was working something out for him and his people that would be to their advantage. God would, as He had done before, "see to it." He was Jehovah-jireh; He would provide. Joseph rested in that. He was entering upon his postgraduate education in the right way and with the right spirit.

Lesson for Us

Turning away from Joseph for the time, we will find it helpful to look quickly at lessons which the narrative should teach us. The whole intriguing account is not merely for the purpose of spinning a yarn. There are valuable lessons hidden in it that should not be missed. Certainly we should have impressed upon us the uncertainties of life that face us daily. Who knows what a day will bring about? Joseph sets out on an errand for his father and fully expects to return from it shortly and resume the normal and routine duties of home life. Instead of that, he never again returns to his father's encampment, and more than twenty years pass before he sees his father again.

Such uncertainties are not peculiar to Joseph. They are ours as well. There are those today who lightly part with loved ones in the morning, expecting to be reunited with them in the evening, but who never again see them. There are street accidents, sudden outbreaks of fire, panics in crowded places, railroad collisions with great loss of life, or sudden illnesses that result in death. These things and many others are occurring on all sides. It is not always the expected, the planned-for that happens. We have before us constantly the demonstration of the truthfulness and accuracy of the old saying "It is the unexpected that happens."

What then? Must we always go about timorously and with darkened hearts under the shadow of dread uncertainty? Not at all. That would make our lives constantly wretched and fearful, and our loving God does not want us to live in such a fashion. The uncertainties of life in the midst of which we all live and indeed always live should, as they did Joseph, turn us to God. We should hold ourselves in readiness at all times to adjust to the circumstances that God allows to come to us, knowing that our times are in His hand and that nothing can happen to us except as it comes through His benevolent and controlling hand. We must learn the supremely important lesson of living one day at a time, not borrowing trouble because of life's uncertainties, realizing that "sufficient unto the day is the evil thereof." We should allow God to teach us to finish each day's work in its own day, for God has said, "Boast not thyself of tomorrow; for thou knowest not what a day may bring forth."

FROM CANAAN TO EGYPT

Sin Multiplies Itself

This narrative should teach us, too, how sin multiplies itself when once yielded to. It grows with indulgence. At the beginning Joseph's brothers were merely envious; then they were jealous; jealousy led to hatred; hatred deepened and got out of control until ultimately it led to cruelty and contemplated murder. One sin does not stop with being one sin. It leads to another sin, and that to still another. Envy, as in this case, goes on to contemplated murder. Nor does it stop there. It does not stop at all, as we shall see. Contemplated murder and the sale of their brother into slavery led on to falsehood and long years of deception.

There is another and a most important lesson we should learn from this narrative. It is that men cannot overthrow or defeat or thwart the purposes and plans of God. When they set themselves to do so, it turns out that quite unintentionally and altogether apart from their consciousness the only thing they accomplish is to help His plans forward to fulfillment. Joseph's brothers were sure that when they sold him into slavery they had made the fulfillment of his dreams impossible, and they gleefully congratulated one another. But that is not at all what they had done. Rather, what they had done was to push their brother one step onward toward his elevation. But they did not know it. They only came to learn it nearly a quarter of a century later.

Working Together for Good

Here is the marvelous working of God. Reuben thought it was wholly his idea that Joseph be not killed but put into the pit. He had his own plans. Judah thought it was his own idea to suggest that Joseph be sold to the Ishmaelites. He had his own plans. The brothers' malice and hatred and deadly animosity were their own. They were under no compulsion. But the God of heaven who also has His own plans took the whole complicated situation of the differing plans of men, together with their envy, jealousy, cruelty, callousness, and hatred, and made them come out to the furtherance of His own benevolent purpose—made them all work together for good. That is a good lesson to learn and to take through life.

There is another lesson that should impress itself upon us from this narrative. It is that we do not rid ourselves of our responsibilities by putting them out of sight. The brothers thought that when they sold Joseph into slavery they had finished with him altogether. How wrong they were they came to learn long years afterward. They were not done with him. They had to face him again. They were held accountable for their treatment of him. They thought they never would be, but they were. There will be a sad reckoning in days to come for every shirked responsibility.

With one more observation about a helpful lesson to be learned we will take our leave of Joseph and let him continue his painful way in chains to Egypt and slavery. But we will look in on him there later. I would have you think again of the uncertainties of life, and our lack of knowledge of what the days ahead may bring to us. And I would have you believe that it is best that way. It is better not to know than to know what tomorrow holds for us. If we knew, we would in all likelihood spoil the plan God has for us.

The Future Hidden

Suppose that when Joseph started out over the fields at his father's bidding he had known what was to happen to him. Suppose he had known how his brothers would meet him, how they would treat him, what they would do to him. Suppose he had known of their hatred, of their determination to slay him, of the pit, of his loneliness, of his sale to the Ishmaelites, of his slavery. Can anyone doubt that if he had known, he would have shrunk back, he would have been terrified, he would not have gone? He would have remained at home, safe and secure. He would not have ventured away from the shelter of his father's protection.

And if that had happened, if he had not gone, oh, what a glorious story would have been spoiled! What a glorious destiny ruined!

No, it is better not to know what lies ahead. It is best to leave the days to come in the capable and kindly hands of the all-knowing, the all-wise, the all-powerful, the everywhere-present God, who loves us and whose purposes regarding us are benevolent and far wiser and better than any we can form for ourselves. Moreover, one of His names is Jehovah-jireh, "the Lord will provide." It is best for us to learn to let Him "see to it." He will—always.

CHAPTER 9

To Egypt and Slavery

M ANY a caravan from the East had made its slow way into Egypt,
bearing merchandise and slaves. One came now that would have
a greater influence on this great nation than any other it had welcomed.
With this one there was a slave lad, sold away from his people, who were
shepherds in Canaan; shepherds—despised by all Egyptians. Egypt did
not know it, and certainly it was not known by the slave boy, but he who
was entering Egypt now with wondering eyes was in thirteen short years
destined to become "lord of all Egypt." Incredible as that seems, it was
nevertheless true.

The land to which the motherless youth came to be sold as a slave
was the possession of the most powerful nation of its time. It had reached
a higher degree of civilization than any other. It was the oldest of nations.
It was first in most of the liberal arts. It had a settled government and
established laws. Its people had built great cities and carried on a thriv-
ing agriculture. Even when Joseph's caravan entered Egypt, the great
pyramid had been built. It proved the people's proficiency in mechanics.
They were acquainted with hieroglyphic writing and were slowly advancing toward an alphabet.

It was to such a land that the poor Hebrew lad, Joseph, was brought.
He must have looked about him in wonder at the magnificent architec-
ture of the great cities, and at the thronging flow of people through the
streets. He must have wondered, too, about the purpose of God in bringing him to this greatest of the nations. What could he possibly accomplish in a mass of humanity such as this? Especially in such a lowly and
humiliating position as that in which he found himself.

He was a slave, fettered to other slaves. He was shortly to be exposed
with his fellow slaves for sale in the open market. There was no one in

all Egypt in a lower position than himself. What could be his mission in this land?

To the Slave Mart

He was brought to the slave mart. He was bought and led away by the man whose property he now was to be—Potiphar, an officer of Pharaoh and "captain of the guard." He was a man of property and of high station, a court officer, an officer of great responsibility. Joseph's confidence in God was unshaken, and he still held to his belief that God intended to use him to carry out some important purpose. When he saw his destination and was charged with his duties he made up his mind to accept the situation as coming from God and helpfully to adapt himself to his new circumstances.

Whenever my thoughts turn to the entrance of Joseph into Egypt and then go forward to what this came to mean, not only to himself but to both Egypt and the children of Israel, my mind turns to the words of John's Gospel in which he writes, "There was a man sent from God" (John 1:6). If ever a man was sent from God, it was Joseph.

It is not difficult for us to think that the great leaders mentioned in the Bible—Moses, Joshua, Daniel, David, Solomon, Isaiah, Jeremiah, and many others—were God-sent men. We find it easy to look upon Cyrus, Alexander, Caesar, Charlemagne, Washington, Lincoln, as men of destiny, raised up to accomplish great tasks. We are all acquainted with great names, outstanding reputations, men of such notable achievements as to make all other renown quite provincial, even contemptible. But a shepherd boy sold into slavery! God-sent! It seems incredible.

All Men Sent From God

What I would have you believe is that every man is sent from God. All persons born into the world are born with some purpose to fulfill, with a mission to accomplish. Human life is not meaningless. Joseph believed that to be true of himself. It was this belief that held him steadfast and courageous through the days and the years that stretched between the slave days and the time of his exaltation, notwithstanding the disheartening experiences that came to him one after another.

It is this belief that will do the same for you. It is a belief that every child of God is justified in making his own, for it is equally as true of you as it was of Joseph. He was a man sent of God. So are you.

50

TO EGYPT AND SLAVERY

One of the great conquerors of ancient times was Cyrus, king of Persia, who overthrew Babylon and made himself master of the world. If you will turn in your Bible to Isaiah 45:1-6, you will see that more than 100 years before Cyrus was born, God had named him, appointed the work he was to do, and authorized and commissioned him to accomplish it. He was a man of destiny.

Something of the same kind can be discerned of most great characters. Jesus recognized it of Himself and gave it expression in the words "To this end was I born, and for this cause came I into the world." Abraham was called out of Ur, of the Chaldean land, for the accomplishment of a most specific purpose. Joseph, years after he entered Egypt as a slave, gave expression to the same truth when he said to his brothers, "It was not you that sent me hither, but God." Paul was said by God to be His "chosen vessel" to take the gospel to the Gentiles.

A Sense of Mission

All persons may have this consciousness of God's call, a sense of mission, of destiny. There is a definite life plan, divinely shaped, for every human being. Each of us is meant to do some exact thing, and the circumstances of our lives are designed to prepare us for its accomplishment. The true significance and glory of our lives will be the doing of the thing that God has marked out for us.

Most men, however, never think of such a thing for themselves. Life has no meaning for them. They feel themselves to be without sufficient importance for the Sovereign of the world to have a special work for them. If you will bring yourself to believe that God has a plan for your life, to make it yours, it will exalt your life immeasurably.

And you should be able to bring yourself to believe it, for it is the God of heaven who declares it to be true. Through His Son He declares He has given "to every man his work." Moreover, in the parables spoken by Jesus it is made plain that for the accomplishment of every man's divinely appointed work, God has given talents to all.

So no matter where you are now, or how obscure or lowly you are, God has a plan for your life. All of the God-sent men and women whose biographies are recorded in the Bible were in their beginnings obscure and insignificant. Think of David among his sheep, of the plowboy Elisha following the oxen, of Nehemiah bearing the cup, of Hannah, wife of

51

Elkanah, of Samuel the temple boy—all of them humble, with lowly stations, yet all with God-planned lives, all of them sent of God, even as you and I.

Your Life Plan

As we take hold of this truth and allow it to sink into our innermost consciousness until it becomes the great conviction of our life we will come to recognize that all that comes to us in the way of surrounding circumstances and experiences has a bearing on God's plan; and is sent to us or allowed to occur to us to mold and shape us better to accomplish the divine purpose. Trials and disappointments, the injuries that enemies and even friends inflict upon us, the hardships of life and its deprivations, the griefs and sorrows we must bear, the heartbreaks and losses we experience, all have their mission from God to prepare us to carry out His plan for our lives. The talents He gives, many or few, the gifts that are ours by nature, the abilities and capacities we acquire, are all from Him and designed to be employed to fulfill our life plan.

Inasmuch, therefore, as this is true, there can never be any place in our lives for despondency, for discouragement. We live in God's thought, and all that enters our lives is for a purpose; and that purpose is a plan of God. How it glorifies all life just to believe that! Our lives will glow with beauty, strength, meaning, and enthusiasm as we make this great truth our own, and learn to abide in God's will.

You may have listened to the coronation ceremonies of one of England's sovereigns. You will have been impressed with the profound religious tone and significance of the proceedings. You may recall the words of the Archbishop of Canterbury as the crown is placed on the head: "George, by the grace of God, King"; "Elizabeth, by the grace of God, Queen." And you may have smiled skeptically at this expression of belief that God had anything to do with choosing the sovereign.

But no smile is called for. The expression "by the grace of God," meaning by divine choice and arrangement, *is* true of sovereigns, but it is *equally* true of you.

By the Grace of God

It would be equally true to say, "Douglas McKane, by the grace of God, colporteur"; "Ruth Burgess, by the grace of God, nurse"; "James Ellis, by the grace of God, teacher"; "John Applegate, by the grace of

God, farmer"; "Harriet Robinson, by the grace of God, housewife." Why should not a farmer or a nurse be one by the grace of God, with a God-planned life, as well as a king, a priest, or a prophet?

The man or woman, the boy or girl, who enters life with that spirit and conviction can go forward, fronting any storm, facing any hardship, meeting any disappointment, rising above any injustice, and keeping the assurance longed for in the lines of the poet:

"Only to know that the path I tread
Is the path marked out for me."

The recognition and embracing of this truth that God has called us and given us a mission, and that we are God-sent, operates to quicken the intellect and sustain the powers of mind and heart in the acquisition of knowledge and the exercise of intelligence. The history of mankind is full of remarkable illustrations of the wonderfully quickening power of the consciousness of the connection and fellowship with God in awakening dormant minds and bringing deadened hearts into tune with the Infinite.

A Mission to Accomplish

Think of John Bunyan, a poor, wretched, drunken tinker in the little town of Bedford, England. He was the town sot, unknown, uncared for. Bunyan did not dream, and certainly no one who knew him could imagine, that he had a brain worth cultivating. But suddenly this man was brought under sharp conviction of sin against God. He felt, as he had never felt before, his accountability to God. Under the stress and impulsion of that new feeling, he turned to Jesus Christ for forgiveness. He was happily converted from his sins to a new way of life, a new consciousness of his relationship to God, a new conviction that God had a work for him to do and a mission to accomplish.

What was the effect? It was like taking a rough, shaggy bulb that has been shut close for months in the grip of winter, and thrusting it into a warm, congenial soil, with the sun and rain ever wooing it from the sky, until it bursts its wrappings and springs forth into a beautiful, fragrant, vigorous life, the life of a lily.

Even so, the dormant, drink-besotted intellect of Bunyan was changed. There came to him such development of powers, such surging of intellect, as neither he nor his neighbors imagined was possible for him. He dreamed dreams. He saw visions. And what dreams; what visions! He translated them into simple and beautiful and moving language that men study today for literary style.

No doubt is in my mind that some whose eyes are following these words, and who do not dream of possessing powers above the average, would be astonished if they were to turn to God with sincere repentance for sin and a sincere desire to know and do the will of God for them—and seek in loving devotion to live the life God has marked out for them —to find how much intellectual power is lying dormant in them and what splendid powers they have inherited, powers that have never come to light but which will in the new heavenly warmth of fellowship with God burst their wrappings and blossom into virtuous and helpful life. They will never know what stupendous potentialities and possibilities are in them until they give themselves completely to do God's will in reverent love and surrender.

This Joseph had done. And as he entered upon his life of slavery in a foreign land, surrounded by strange people and facing unknown trials, his young heart went out to and rested in the great God of his people, the God who had led and protected his ancestors and who he was sure was now leading and protecting him. With that he was content. He wanted only to know what God's further will was for him. Nor did he have long to wait.

CHAPTER 10

From Slave to Overseer

I T WAS by no easy steps that Joseph came to the exalted station he at last reached. Rather, it was by a series of hardships and misadventures, of hazards and conflicts, of disappointments and heartbreak. And when we come to the end of his story and look back over the way he had come, and over the many stages of his career, we can see that the difficulties faced, the postponements of expectations, the trying situations passed through, the outrageous injustice suffered, had not only put Joseph to the proof but also were the very means by which (met with patient endurance and righteous endeavor, as they were) all that was manly and strong and tender in his character was brought out and ripened. It was by this process that he was conditioned and prepared for the great work for which he was destined.

During the years of his early life Joseph had been brought up in surroundings that had sheltered him from hardship and trouble. He had been shielded from grinding toil and cruel insult. He was the favorite son of his father, who lavished upon him every luxury. He was now removed from those conditions and had met the blazing hatred and murderous animosities of his brothers. He had been cast into a pit to die, and then sold into ignominious slavery.

In that slavery he was taken into a land new and strange to him. In this land he had not one friend in the whole country. He had no knowledge of the language men were speaking all about him. He had no knowledge of and no training in any trade that would make him of any value in Egypt. He was stripped of everything but his own manhood, his faith in God, his implicit confidence that God had chosen him to be of service. It was a most disheartening and dispiriting introduction to the new land he had entered and the new life he was to begin.

When Character Is Revealed

When any man is chafed by injustice, stung by injury, and galled by cruelty, his real character emerges in the attitude he assumes toward his surroundings, toward men and toward life generally. If a man is by nature weak, he will, when he is deceived and cruelly injured, become morose and suddenly surrender all hope of anything good. He is likely to vent his spleen on all about him and angrily denounce the heartlessness and cruelties of men.

If, however, a man is by nature proud, he will be inclined to gather himself up and fight his way back from every blow, watching narrowly and working determinedly to discover his way to an adequate revenge.

If a man, moreover, is mean by nature, he is likely to accept his fate, but endeavor to relieve his hurt by indulging in cynical, spiteful, and stinging remarks about the frailties and failures of human life, unable to see good in anything or anybody, while at the same time greedily seeking and accepting the paltriest rewards he can obtain.

Joseph's nature, however, was neither weak nor proud nor mean, and the convictions that grew from his dreams and his confidence in the God of his fathers saved him from any impulse to react in any of these unfortunate ways against the experiences that came to him. The supreme wholesomeness of his nature, as well as the daily blessings of God that followed him, enabled him to meet his troubles with patience, to resist the influences that would drive him to despair, and preserved him from every sort of morbid attitude toward the world and life.

The Midianite traders who had bought Joseph from his brethren finally reached Egypt. They took him to some slave market, where he was exposed for sale together, perhaps, with scores or even hundreds more. The others, no doubt, were from the regions of the Upper Nile and of Central Africa, which were then, as they were for centuries later, the sources of supply for the heartless and inhuman slave traffic.

Chief of the Royal Police

The delicately complexioned Joseph must have stood out conspicuously among the swarthy sons and daughters of the more tropical lands. The man who bought him was Potiphar, "the captain of the guard." He was, if Young's Literal Translation is followed here, "head of the executioners." Some would have it "chief marshal"; others "provost marshal";

still others "master of the horse." Scholarly Dr. Kitto, in his *Bible History of the Holy Land,* wrote of him as "chief of the royal police." His words are—

"Potiphar was undoubtedly the chief of the executioners; but this is a high office in the East as a court office, for such executioners have nothing to do with execution of the awards of the law in its ordinary course, but only with those of the king. It is thus an office of great responsibility; and to insure its proper execution, it is entrusted to an officer of the court, who has necessarily under his command a body of men whose duty it is to preserve the order and peace of the palace and its precincts, to attend and guard the royal persons on public occasions, and under the direction of their chief to inflict such punishment as the king awards upon those who incur his displeasure. . . . A functionary who combined these various duties in his person cannot perhaps be better described than by the title 'Chief of the royal police.'"

Potiphar's position was, therefore, one of highest responsibility as the guardian of the sovereign. He was an Egyptian grandee, or member of the Egyptian aristocracy, exalted both in his office and in the favor of the king. Without doubt his residence, manned by many slaves, was one of those magnificent and spacious palaces that the spade of the archeologist has disclosed covered with hieroglyphs. You can imagine how his newest slave, accustomed to the simplicities of a pastoral home and the tendernesses of a loving father, must have looked about him with trembling and trepidation as he passed through the sphinx-guarded gates of the pillared avenue that led into the recesses of this vast, strange Egyptian palace. Everybody there communicated with one another in a strange language, and everything about him was new and different.

God's Presence and Protection

Notwithstanding this strangeness, he did not lose the sense of the presence and protection of his father's God. It flooded his soul and stilled his restless thoughts, and kept him in perfect peace. The record is that "the Lord was with Joseph." Joseph in Egypt was better off, though he may have found it hard to believe, than his brothers in Canaan with a blood-stained garment in their hands and a consciousness of guilt upon their souls. He was sustained by thoughts of the God he had been taught to love and revere. Crowding back into his mind came the stories told

57

him by Isaac and by Jacob. His great-grandsire Abraham had also been called away from his home to carry out the purposes of God. His own father, Jacob, had passed through the experience of being an exile, a fugitive, banished from his home. He recalled the vision of which Jacob had told him when he had fled his father Isaac's tent. In the time of his greatest need the angels of God had come to him, and he had seen them on the shining staircase that connected earth with heaven. Moreover, the voice of God had come to him, encouraging him with the assurance of guidance, comfort, and protection. Great promises had been made to Jacob in his extremity, and Joseph knew that they had been fulfilled.

These stories of the dealings of God with his ancestors had been deeply etched into the memory of Joseph, and they served now to encourage him and keep him strong, and to enable him to meet the new conditions and possibilities into which he had so suddenly been plunged. He brought them all vividly before him. He did not doubt that his father's God would be his God and give to him the same guidance, the same protection, and the same deliverance He had never failed to give Abraham, Isaac, and Jacob.

He Would Be True to God

As he thought of these things he reached the decision to place himself wholly in the hands of the Keeper of Israel, who had always safeguarded his ancestors. He too would be true to God in this land of his exile. He too would follow the leading of Jehovah-jireh, the God who would provide, who would "see to it." He was sure that God had not lost control of his affairs, that near at hand in this darkness of slavery God was keeping watch over him and would shape events and bring them out for His own glory. He was thrilled to the soul as he committed himself in high resolve to find the Lord's will in all this, and to carry it out with diligence and faithfulness. His heart would be undivided in its allegiance and service to the God of heaven. The trials that were his lot in this condition of slavery he would meet with fortitude. The duties required of him he would perform with fidelity.

Thus, instead of crushing him and bringing him to despair, the injustices and calamities that came to Joseph led him in a completely opposite direction. The pampered boy had been transformed into a man, and a man who was thoughtful, courageous, and wholly self-possessed.

He firmly believed that God had a mission for him to perform, a task to accomplish. Joseph was going somewhere, and now he was on his way. To face up to life in that spirit makes an enormous difference in what you do with life and what life does with you.

It was indeed a *man* that God sent into Egypt to prepare the way for His people. In this simple way David describes the event. "He sent a *man* before them, even Joseph, who was sold for a servant: whose feet they hurt with fetters: he was laid in iron: until the time that his word came: the word of the Lord tried him" (Ps. 105:17-19). He was no longer a boy, the pet of a doting father. A few days of trouble, cruelty, and wrong had brought out the man in him. Now he was ready for what was coming. He was a *man,* a *true* man, a *stalwart* man, a *God-sent* man, a *fearless* man, because he knew God was with him.

Surrounded by Idolatry

As Joseph entered upon his new life it should not be overlooked that he was surrounded on every side by idolatry. This exposed him to temptations of an extraordinary influence. False gods were worshiped with the accompaniment of pomp and splendor supported by wealth and culture. Notwithstanding this, Joseph, fortified by his faith in God, was able to preserve his simplicity and his fidelity to God. Nor did he attempt to hide his own principles. He was not ashamed of his religious convictions or of the worship of the true God.

That kind of devotion is bound to have the same results wherever it is manifested. The record is: "And the Lord was with Joseph, and he was a prosperous man. . . . And his master saw that the Lord was with him, and that the Lord made all that he did to prosper in his hand." Potiphar was impressed as he observed Joseph. His confidence in him was enlarged as day followed day. He finally gave him control of his entire estate and household, making Joseph his steward, manager of all he owned. "And he left all that he had in Joseph's hand; and he knew not ought he had, save the bread which he did eat."

"The Lord was with Joseph, and he was a prosperous man." An old version has a quaint translation here. It is "The Lord was with Joseph, and he was a luckie fellow!" Something here seems quite incongruous; these two things do not seem to belong together. But the meaning plainly is that the things Joseph did, the things entrusted to him by his master, came out well. Everything he did prospered, was successful. And the reason for that was that "the Lord was with" him. His shadow did not follow him more closely or more persistently than did success. Potiphar and Potiphar's entire household acquired the habit of expecting that this young Hebrew slave could solve all problems, untie every knot, disentangle every snarl, in the complex activities and routine affairs of a large household and estate, and bring even the most intricate arrangements to a successful issue.

The Secret of His Prosperity

The secret of this remarkable prosperity was twofold. First was the fact, as has already been mentioned, that while Joseph had been stripped of his princely coat, he had not been stripped of his princely character. He had retained his integrity and his confidence in God. He had not allowed himself to go sour. He was industrious, alert, prompt, diligent, obedient, and trustworthy. His fellow slaves might loiter and squander their time and the time of their master; Joseph packed every moment with activity. The others might be satisfied to do surface work alone. Not Joseph. He was thorough, skillful. He did not do his work merely to avoid a frown or a beating. He did his work first of all to win the approval of his heavenly Master, whose eye he believed was always upon him, before whom he constantly stood. The man who lives consciously in the presence of God will always prosper, always be "a luckie fellow."

The prosperity, therefore, that marked everything Joseph did was not the consequence of a divine miracle. Rather, his meticulous care in doing his work well, his conscientious interest in his master's welfare, brought the blessing of Heaven upon what he did. Joseph knew that his success was because of the favor of God. Even Potiphar accepted that explanation as the secret of the amazing prosperity that accompanied all that Joseph did. "His master saw that the Lord was with him, and that the Lord made all that he did to prosper in his hand." The result was that Potiphar "left all that he had in Joseph's hand; and he knew not ought he had, save the bread which he did eat."

CHAPTER 11

In Tune With the Infinite

JOSEPH remained in Potiphar's household for ten years. His fidelity and the blessing of God upon him was such that the time came when Potiphar looked upon him no longer as a slave, but rather as a son, and treated him as such, placing the management of all he had under Joseph's supervision.

"He was a prosperous man." I linger at this point because it seems so rich in meaning and contains such valuable lessons. Many are the ways in which the Lord is with His servants. Many are the ways in which He prospers them. It may not be, and indeed it seldom is, by an outward symbol. It is not by a visible badge that can be seen and read—nothing like the wearing of a cross made of gold or the making of the sign of the cross. God often is with a man in the suggestion of thought, in the impression of the mind, in the prompting of a choice, in the leading to a decision, in the resolution of the will, in the upsurge of high, noble, heavenly feeling, in the direction of his steps, in the selection of his words, supplying him with the right answer at the right time in the midst of the right circumstances. God prospers a man by giving him the schooling that cannot be obtained in any institution of learning, training him for God's special purposes by methods and processes that human schools never dreamed of, thus making him a fit instrument for the work God has destined him to do. Ideas as well as money are gifts of God. Suggestions in management and administration, delivering thoughts in times of extremity, promptings to silence when it is better than words, guidance in words when they will do more than silence—all these are gifts bestowed by the Divine Spirit upon men who are fully given up to do the will of the Lord.

A God-centered Life

Joseph was a slave under Potiphar. Nevertheless, the Lord was with him and he was a prosperous man. No child of God can be placed in such difficulties and surroundings that he is beyond the reach and outside the area of the blessing of the Lord. There are no circumstances that can prevent the prosperity that God gives. Looked at through the eyes of a man without spiritual discernment, it would not appear that Joseph was a prosperous man. He was a slave. He was in bondage. He was a piece of property. His time did not belong to himself. He had no liberty of action or of choice. He was cut off from his father and from his home. Nevertheless, the Lord was with him and he was a prosperous man.

The secret was that his life was centered in God. It was not centered in self. It was not centered in circumstances. It was not centered in surroundings. It was not centered in external things. When men live in external things there can be no real prosperity even in the midst of riches. When a man must total up his bank savings and his stocks and bonds in order to determine whether he is prosperous and whether he can really enjoy himself, such a man is without any real understanding of what comprises true joy or of what constitutes real prosperity. Men who live in and by their bank books and the things of the world about them have no real conception of what it is to live. Man cannot live by bread alone, or by gold or things of the external senses. Life is not an outward thing; it is a thing of the inner spirit. When a man finds it impossible to live within himself and draw sustenance from the things of the Spirit, then he does not live at all in the truest sense of the word. He becomes a shuttlecock of every changing circumstance, a plaything of shifting surroundings. Any clatter of a telegraph key can then bring down upon him the wreck of his hopes; any shrilling of the telephone can bring an end to his empire of dreams. The rainy day from which he has endeavored to safeguard himself can unsettle his whole life and bring darkness and despair to all his future.

Joseph did not live in external circumstances. If he had, his days would have been spent in tears, his nights in despair. He lived in God. He fed on hope. God was at his right hand. All his expectation was in God. "The Lord was with Joseph." He lived a religious life, a devoted life. He lived in God, with God, for God. He walked with God. He identified the very life of his soul with God.

IN TUNE WITH THE INFINITE

No Slave to Circumstances

Circumstances had no sovereignty over him. They did not control him. They were under his feet. He rose above them. He might be a slave to Potiphar, but he was no slave to circumstances. He used them; they did not use him. That is the kind of man he was. And when you know that of a man, you have the key to his whole life. If a man is rightly related to God, his whole life is sure, safe, determined. The disturbances of his outer life—its inequalities, its distractions, injustices, and cruelties—do not unsettle him. Assurance guards his heart notwithstanding outward turbulence; light and peace govern his mind despite the outrageous bludgeonings of unjust circumstance. The great crises of his life do not move him away from his moorings in God. It then is possible for him to be an exile, a slave, separated from father and home and friendship and still be a prosperous man, "a luckie fellow." Such was Joseph. The man in him, centered in God, was deeper than the slave. It enabled him to rise above his slavery and live in another world—the world of the Spirit, the world of God, the veritable kingdom of heaven.

We must not leave this phase of Joseph's experience without noticing a thing of supreme importance. It is a part of the record that "his master saw that the Lord was with him, and that the Lord made all that he did to prosper in his hand" (Gen. 39:3). That is a truly wonderful thing. A man whose life is God-centered has something about him that is not found in any other man. Irreligious men observe that God is with him, and they are influenced. His manner of life impresses them, even heathen men, even idolaters as was Potiphar, far more than anything that could be said. They may not hear a word, but they see a life and are moved thereby. Our relationship to heaven, our standing with God; the convictions that control our lives, our religious beliefs; can be seen and are seen by men about us—irreligious men, godless men, all men. That is something to keep in mind.

A Religious Life Never a Hidden Life

The true God was not known to Potiphar. But this idolater saw something in his Hebrew slave, this lad of fair countenance and cheerful spirit, that he had not seen in anyone else. The higher life in a man, the truly religious life, the life centered in God, is never an unseen life. It

63

shines through. It cannot be hidden. It makes itself known and felt. Potiphar did not see that the Lord was with Joseph because Joseph said so or because Joseph made long religious speeches. He did not see that the Lord was with him because Joseph argued with him about the errors of his idolatrous beliefs and criticized his heathen practices. Nor because Joseph took pains to explain to him who the true God is and the right way to worship. No, Potiphar saw that the Lord was with him because all that he did prospered. He reasoned from the things he saw to the things unseen. The unbroken prosperity that attended everything Joseph did meant something. There must be a reason. There was no explanation for such a state of affairs but a religious reason. It must be found in the slave's relationship to the Deity he worshiped. This man was the servant of Jehovah. And Jehovah approved of him and therefore prospered him in all his undertakings.

How far is it possible for us to mingle among men, to work alongside men, to be any man's servant, employee, friend, associate, and conceal that at the very least there is a God whom we serve? How long have you been in the service of your employer, lived next door to your neighbor, dealt daily with your tradesman, fellowshiped constantly with your friend, without his learning about your faith in the God you serve and the truth you believe? How can these things be concealed when a man has God in his life and heart? There are, you must know, subtleties of movement, of expression, of looks, certain mysteries of conduct, that men explain only on the grounds of religion, only because we live our lives by standards and ideals that come from above, from the God we serve. There are persons in whose presence you cannot spend five minutes without being better for it and knowing you have been blessed. That is the way it was with Joseph. Potiphar saw that the Lord was with him. That is the way it may be with you. That is the way it should be with everyone who truly serves the God of heaven.

When God truly dwells with a man and a man truly gives himself to serve God, this service will be known to others than the man himself. God's presence in a life manifests itself in ways that are not hidden, but open for all to see. It may be in the expression of the countenance, the glance of the eye, the tone of the voice, the small courtesies of life, in helpful, gracious conduct—all little things, but freighted with meaning that can be easily interpreted.

Some men shed light about them. They even speak light. Some men shame us when we do anything in their presence that is mean or cowardly or sneaking or unworthy or questionable or offensive. Their character shines through. They may not speak a word; they may only look. They do not need to preach or condemn. Without any of that, we know instantly and intuitively something of their sincerity and nobility. We recognize, as Potiphar did of Joseph, that the Lord is with them.

One Man Blessed Because of Another

There is another point we should notice before we pass on to Joseph's later experiences. It is that the blessings God gave to Joseph did not stop with Joseph. The prosperity that came to the slave was shared by the master. The record is "And it came to pass from the time that he had made him overseer in his house, and over all that he had, that the Lord blessed the Egyptian's house for Joseph's sake; and the blessing of the Lord was upon all that he had in the house, and in the field" (Gen. 39:5).

For the sake of one man, another man is blessed. The blessing on one man's faithfulness rubs off on another man. You will not be wasting time if you give some thought to that. A man may look at his prosperity and conclude that he must be favored of God, when all the time his prosperity may be because of the fidelity of a humble servant in his employ, an associate or partner in his business, a devoted companion in his home, to whom he has never dreamed of attributing his good fortune. In Potiphar's case it was a master blessed because of a good slave. And he knew it. Many today do not know it. With smug complacency they consider and count their blessings, and are convinced that these benefits came to them as a result of their own skill and ability and smartness. A man looks upon himself as a genius in business—shrewd, wide-awake, alert, knowing when to move and when not to. All this prosperity is, he reasons, the reward of his own superior capabilities. He would be outraged to be told that it really is the reward of the devotion and fidelity of some servant or some associate devoted to his welfare, filling some lowly place of responsibility.

There is many a man blessed and prospered and safeguarded from disaster because he has the good fortune, without recognizing it, of having a praying wife. He never attends church himself—too busy making a living; religion is for women and children; he has to make the living for them all. But his wife does not miss church, does not fail to pray for him. He does not know that his prosperity is due, all of it, to his neglected, praying wife, whose religion he scorns and flouts. She never stops praying for him. If she should, the judgments of heaven might fall upon him. He knows nothing of all this. He fails to recognize that his blessings come because of his faithful wife. It is not his sagacity, his genius, that is the source of his prosperity. It is his praying wife.

The Preserving Salt of the Earth

So in every age the righteous servants of God have been the salt of the earth. God blesses one man for the sake of another, as he blessed Potiphar for the sake of Joseph. Ten godly men in Sodom would have preserved the lives of all the godless people of that godless city. A husband is blessed because of the godliness of his wife. A man whose crops are rich and abundant is blessed because he has a little crippled, praying girl in his house who believes in God and prays for her father, and thus connects that house with heaven. Everything he owns he owes to her. And he does not know it.

Always it has been so. The righteous, the true, the loving, the God fearing, are not only the preserving salt of the earth; they are also the light of the world. Without them the world would by now be nothing but a burned-out cinder flying through space. Without them God would long ago have crushed this little planet, pulverized it, and blown it away on the winds of His wrath. It is men of prayer, men of God, who have kept it going. It was the presence of Paul in the vessel on the storm-lashed sea that saved all aboard. It is the presence of God's servants that preserves the earth from the lightning showers of judgment. And as we have seen, it was because of Joseph that the house of Potiphar was blessed. Moreover, in Potiphar's case he had sense enough to discern that fact and to acknowledge it.

And thus Joseph's God-centered life put him and kept him in tune with God. Such a life is bound to shed blessing on all who touch it, as it did in Joseph's case. So it will be with every person whose life is centered in God.

CHAPTER 12

Years of Valuable Schooling

NOT only did the years of slavery in Potiphar's establishment result in blessing and prosperity to this Egyptian court official; they were also of enormous benefit to Joseph. They provided him an education, a training, and a preparation for his lifework, his career as Egyptian prime minister.

Joseph gave himself to do the will of God quite early in life, as we have seen. Nor did the unfolding developments of his experience bring any change in his determination to be true to the God of his fathers. His decision had been made. His resolution was fixed. His life was lived in the consciousness of God's presence. In every relationship of life, in every decision he was required to make, he did not fail to consult the will of God regarding his attitudes and his conduct. It was because of this that he was a prosperous man. God cares for and honors the man who keeps close fellowship with Him and seeks always to know and do His will.

Through the years of his servitude in Potiphar's house this was Joseph's way of life. His master's confidence in his integrity and ability enlarged constantly. Potiphar placed ever greater responsibility upon this Hebrew youth. The time came when he gave him charge of his whole estate and all his affairs, including the management of his residential palace and its daily requirements and routine.

Contact With Important Personages

In this capacity, as the major-domo of a great establishment, Joseph was brought into contact constantly with important personages. Men high in the affairs of government were visitors in Potiphar's palace—men of rank, men of learning, men of science, men of religion, men of the priesthood, counselors of the Pharaoh, officers of various state departments and bureaus, men responsible for the conduct and administration of public affairs, as well as personages of exalted social station.

In his position of responsibility as manager of household affairs it fell to Joseph's lot to plan for and carry through the arrangements for these gatherings and banquets, conferences and social affairs. Thus he came to learn much of Egyptian public life, of Egyptian politics, of Egyptian learning and culture and social life, and of what was going on in the great world about him. He was in this atmosphere and in these activities a number of years before the crash came that swept him out of it all and brought him to disgrace and imprisonment.

During these rewarding years he developed and matured in every way. He learned much from the conversations he heard, from the discussions carried forward in his hearing, in his association with men of high station, even though he was in a state of servitude. His alert faculties and active mind busied themselves with great matters; he became aware of the causes that produced certain effects in the nation; he learned much about the ways by which men were governed, the way they were influenced and swayed in definite directions. He came to understand more and more about economic, social, and political affairs. Indeed, Potiphar's house became a helpful school to Joseph and provided him with a remarkably broad education and preparation for the immense responsibilities of prime minister of this greatest nation of its time.

No Accident That Joseph Was in Potiphar's House

Without doubt, this was the reason Joseph had been placed where he was, and why he had been prospered to the point that brought him this important opportunity. It was no accident that he had been sold into slavery. It was no accident that he had been put on the slave block. It was no accident that he had been bought by Potiphar. It was no accident that he had been prospered in Potiphar's service, and had been promoted to the management of Potiphar's household. In all of this there is evidence of design, of a divine plan. These years of servitude in Potiphar's house were not wasted years for Joseph. Indeed, nothing that was allowed to come to him—though much of it seemed outrageously unjust, uncalled for, and cruel—was without benefit to him.

This is the way it always is with the true child of God. His times are in God's hands. The things that happen to him do not just happen. There is purpose in them. They do not come by chance. There is meaning in them. They are allowed and they are designed to accomplish something. And always what they are designed to do is for the benefit of the child of God. They are not meant to injure; they are meant to bless.

Joseph Was Not Hurt

So it was with Joseph. Being put into the pit did not hurt him. Unpleasant, yes. Frightening, certainly. But not really hurtful. Being sold into slavery did not hurt him. It was not actually a calamity but rather an opportunity. Being bought as a piece of merchandise was humiliating, but not really hurtful. Joseph suffered no loss from it. On the contrary, great gain came to him from it. Nothing can ever hurt the man who has given himself to follow God. His life is in God's hand, and everything that happens to him must come through the hand of God, and therefore by the permission of God. And everything that comes through the hand of God and is permitted to touch the lives of His servants is shaped and fashioned by that hand to bless, not to harm.

It is true that there is a Scripture expression that speaks of Joseph's feet being hurt in his later experience of imprisonment. It is in Psalm 105:17 and 18: "He sent a man before them, even Joseph, who was sold for a servant: whose feet they hurt with fetters: he was laid in iron." True, his feet were hurt. But Joseph was more than his feet. In more ways than one, Joseph was above his feet. Joseph was not hurt. Quite possibly his feelings were hurt. But not he himself.

I do not want to leave this important lesson without impressing it deeply upon your thinking. Perhaps this can be done most forcefully by asking you to give play to your imagination. Suppose in the early years, indeed, at the beginning of Joseph's slavery, he had taken things into his own hands, had watched his opportunity to escape, and had done so. Suppose he had been successful in shaking off pursuit and had managed at long last to make his way to Canaan and his father's encampment. We can picture the rejoicing that would have followed. But can we picture some other things? Suppose an escape from slavery, no imprisonment, no forecasting for the butler and baker, no interpretation of Pharaoh's dreams, no exaltation to high rank and high power, no storing up of grain, no saving of life, no going of Jacob's family to Egypt, no land of Goshen, no growing of Israel into a great nation, no deliverance, no giving of the law, no conquest of Canaan, no system of divine worship, no throne of David, no divine promises to David, no Messiah, no Christian church, no ——? Oh, what a change in world affairs would have resulted from the escape of an obscure Hebrew slave in Egypt!

Providential Supervision

One writer years ago let his imagination run wild on a theme similar to this in order to emphasize the providential supervision in the story of Joseph. He wrote a book that presents a man in a higher form of existence, who, looking down on the poor Hebrew lad as he was being taken by the Midianites to Egypt, found his pity for the poor slave awakened. This sympathetic man saw that as Joseph was an alert, ingenious lad with a bold, adventurous spirit, he managed to find a way to escape from the caravan on the first night after his brothers had sold him when the Midianites were not at a great distance from his father's encampment. He had succeeded in getting away from the camp when a yellow dog began to yelp. The men who had him in charge were awakened by the barking of the dog. The escaping slave was recaptured and brought back.

The story proceeds to describe the feelings of the onlooker. He wanted to kill the dog before it had roused Joseph's captors. Joseph would thus have been able to get away on his short journey to his father's home. This would have prevented great sorrow on the part of Jacob, great suffering on the part of Joseph, and exposed the cruelty and duplicity of the brothers; and the ends of justice would have been served all around.

Hands Off

But as the onlooker was about to kill the dog and thus facilitate Joseph's escape, his guardian said, "Hands off." And to impress him with the evils of interfering, he spirited him off to a world where he could do what he thought of doing—kill the dog and help the escape—and could see the results of his intervention. Here he killed the dog, it did not bark, his keepers were not awakened, Joseph got away, and reached home in safety. His father rejoiced; his brothers, at first chagrined, were finally comforted. That seemed a better way than slavery.

But years later, when the famine came on, there was no Joseph in

Egypt to predict it and prepare for it. There was no food laid up in the storehouses. Palestine, Egypt, and other countries were ravaged by famine. Great numbers perished. Those who were spared were destroyed by the savage Hittites. Egypt was blotted out. Civilization was set back centuries. Greece and Rome did not advance beyond barbarism. The history of the entire world was changed. Countless evils ensued—and all because someone whose wisdom was ignorance killed a yellow dog to save a fleeing slave from present trouble, to his own loss, and the terrible loss of the whole world.

And the writer of the imaginative book etches deeply the lesson that it is better to keep our hands off the providences of God. Many a magnificent plan of God's devising has been spoiled by human meddling. You who read the Bible will recall that Peter wanted to prevent Jesus from going to the cross. Suppose he had succeeded in that! Many a time, without doubt, the promptings of love have kept a life from hardship, advised against a sacrifice, saved a person from suffering, without ever considering that at the same time it had blighted a life, marred a destiny, thwarted a plan of God.

Certainly our sympathy goes out to Joseph as he is sold into slavery, as he is humiliated, and later cast into irons and forgotten. But we should not fail to recognize that if human pity at that time could have rescued him and saved him from the ignominy and humiliation and slavery, the glorious finale that followed, with all its blessed service to men of all centuries, would have been lost.

In God's Hands

Joseph, however, made no effort to escape. He left himself in the hands of the Lord. He believed God was leading, even though he could not understand the direction this leading was taking. God would "see to it." He would provide. He always had done so for his ancestors. He would now. He had never failed. He would not fail now. Joseph would leave all things to God. He believed, and he believed rightly, that he was a ward of Jehovah. He accepted the situation in which he found himself, as coming from the Lord. Consequently, he adjusted himself to his environment with a contented mind, doing willingly, and with the best skill he could muster, everything he was required to do.

It had been this attitude on his part that had created his master's confidence in him. It was not long before Potiphar found it to be to his profit to shift more and more responsibility to the hands of this diligent and industrious slave. Finally, as we have seen, he kept nothing back from him, trusting everything in his establishment to Joseph's care. "He left all that he had in Joseph's hand."

It was as a result of this resignation to his lot as coming from the Lord that Joseph found opening before him the valuable opportunities that came to him as the administrator of Potiphar's household. If it was in accordance with the will of God for him to be a slave, he was determined to be content with nothing less than being the best of slaves. What his position required him to do he would do with all his might and all his heart, as doing it unto the Lord. It is this spirit that can turn even slavery into opportunity for advancement and prosperity. A man who meets the experiences of life in that spirit cannot be kept down. Calamities, disappointments, injustices are turned into steppingstones. The man of that spirit learns life's most valuable secret. In the school of Potiphar's home and the prison experience that followed, Joseph learned how to be a prime minister of the world's greatest empire. Better still, he learned how to meet injustice, wrong, cruelty, inhuman treatment, temptation, and misfortune so as to take no harm from them, how to keep his heart sweet and gentle, to keep his mind pure and clean, to keep his spirit brave and strong, and his faith in God bright and clear. A school that provides such an education is of the greatest value. Forever after Joseph must have preserved in his heart a sense of appreciation for his alma mater.

CHAPTER 13

Joseph's Answer to Temptation

AS JOSEPH advanced in years, passing his twenty-first birthday, he also grew in knowledge and sound judgment. He developed rapidly as responsibility after responsibility was placed upon him. He passed swiftly from adolescence to manhood. His features took on an appearance of maturity, but retained much of the grace and charm of youth. Genuine character of superior quality together with beauty of mind and heart usually reflects itself in form and feature and manner. It did not fail to do so in Joseph's case. He was not only a prosperous man; he was an unusually handsome man.

There was a wholesomeness about this slave lad that was most appealing. The tales he had heard in the tents of his father and grandfather had done more than create interest. They had developed a love of obedience. As the conviction grew that he was selected to accomplish some important service for God, it became a part of life itself to carry out most meticulously what he understood to be the will of Jehovah.

There was something most striking about this firmness and earnestness in connection with his religious life, his worship and devotion. The qualities of fidelity, of integrity, of honesty, of truthfulness, and of gentleness characterized all his transactions and dealings, and never changed through his whole life except to grow. That growth made Joseph into a man of fixed, inflexible principle, and that principle was rooted in religion, in his relationship to the God he worshiped and served.

Men Without Standards

There are men—we all know them—who seem to live without principle of any kind. They have no standards of living to which they are true, no ideals to which they adhere, no anchor to hold them and keep them from floating and shifting with the tides and currents of life. They do not hold to a steady and fixed course, but are swayed and drawn from the true course by any influence brought to bear upon them by the allurements and enticements that appeal to the outer senses. They live in the outward things of life, in the senses; their natures are sensual, and they find it possible lightly to cast away the standards by which others govern and control their lives. Not so was Joseph. He was a man who governed his life by principle. His standards were lofty and he did not deviate from them.

He had now been with Potiphar several years. His ability and capacity were such, and his fidelity to the interests of his master was such, that he had risen to the highest post he could expect as a slave. He was the steward, the bailiff, of all that belonged to Potiphar. He was trusted and honored with his master's confidence and even his affection.

Nothing, however, in his present station gave him any expectation that his dreams were about to be fulfilled. Those dreams were much in his mind. They had promised a great future, an elevation to high station, of wide influence, but certainly not in slavery. And there was no discernible prospect before him of anything but continued slavery. Under the unchanging routine of his work in Potiphar's establishment there must have come to him a sense of disappointment that was calculated to depress him. As the years passed, this feeling must have settled down upon him more and more. He did not slacken his efforts in behalf of his master's welfare. His efficiency in the performance of his many tasks did not lessen. But perhaps a heaviness of spirit came to him at intervals as he thought of the promise of his dreams and contrasted that with his actual position.

Looking Down an Alluring Path

It was at this very time that there opened to him a most unexpected opportunity to advance to a high position. He was prompted to look down an alluring and unthought-of path that might prove to be the way by which the promise of his dreams would be realized. Could it be possible that the recognition that had come to him, the advancement he had achieved, the promotion he had been given, were all meant to lead to the opportunity that now opened before him? An intrigue with the wife of his master might possibly lead to the very elevation he thought he had reason to anticipate. It is true he had never dreamed of its coming in such a fashion. But then he had never dreamed of being sold into slavery by his own brothers, those he was led to expect would sometime "make obeisance" to him.

This was no opportunity that he had opened by his own choice. It was nothing he had sought or maneuvered to bring about. It had been forced upon him. It might be something, however, in which there were large possibilities in the direction of the fulfillment of his dreams. Should he continue to wait patiently and passively for God to work out his advancement or should he do what might be in his own power to bring it about? His master's wife had opened to him a course of action that might well be the way to lift him out of the status of a slave. Quite likely he knew that other men had taken such a course without scruple.

It is plain from the record that the temptation that came to Joseph did not appeal to him with overwhelming force from the sensual side. There can be no doubt, however, that it did make some appeal to that side of his nature. He was a man, with a man's nature. He was young, vigorous, virile, with the desires and passions common to all young men. It cannot be doubted that when his master's wife "cast her eyes" upon him and made her approaches to him, and finally came out with her seductive proposal, his lower nature was aroused. However, he was not a passionate man. He was not swept off his feet and overmastered by lust. He resisted. He argued. He endeavored to reason with her, to get her to see why they should not enter upon such a guilty intrigue.

Another Side of His Nature

The appeal to him was to another side of his nature altogether. Here was an unsought opportunity that had come to him—one that might have in it possibilities of great advancement, that could help forward the realization of his dreams. Entering into this intrigue with the woman who had become enamored of him, and who apparently would stop at nothing to obtain the favors she sought of him, held the possibility of his being put in his master's place, the ultimate elimination of Potiphar altogether, and Joseph's elevation to succeed his master in that household. There was nothing in the prevailing state of morality of Egypt that would make this either unlikely or impossible. Moreover, it must have occurred to Joseph that it would be to his advantage to stand well with his master's wife. To please her would promote his interests and do much to secure his advancement. To cross her and refuse to comply with her wishes would make her his foe and possibly ruin his hopes for the future. To yield for the present might obtain for him an influence that he could use later for the best of results. It could put him in a position where he would find it possible to advance the purpose that God was seeking to carry out.

Men have always been prone to so reason, and it is possible that Joseph was tempted to reason thus. This is the reasoning of policy, of expediency. It has always been a traitor to a man's true nature. And always, when pursued, it brings ruin. It would have done so in Joseph's case if he had put policy before principle. Indeed, he might have enlarged his influence in the house of Potiphar. He might have succeeded him in control. But it would not have lasted. And he would never have become what God had in mind for him—the prime minister of Egypt. He never would have accomplished what God planned for him—the salvation and the elevation of his own people.

Day by Day

Potiphar's wife was persistent. She renewed her solicitation, the record says, "day by day." She intended to have her way with this man who "was a goodly person, and well favoured." Doubtless she was not accustomed to being denied, and she did not propose to be denied on this occasion. She wanted Joseph, and Joseph she was determined to have.

In spite of the tumult and turbulence of his own thoughts, Joseph attempted to reason with her. He pointed out what an enormity it would be for him to consent to her proposals. His master, he said, had placed him in a position of trust, of great responsibility. Potiphar did not even know what there was in the house. He had left it all to Joseph. He trusted him. He kept back nothing from him, nothing "but thee, because thou art his wife." It would be an unthinkable wickedness to steal his master's wife, even with her own consent. It would be an appalling breach of trust.

His reasoning made no appeal to Potiphar's wife. Very likely she never heard it. She had no concern for the rightness and wrongness of the matter. She brushed Joseph's reasonings aside. She renewed her urgings. But to no avail. Joseph was beginning to see his course of action, his duty, and in a clear light. As she became more urgent, more insistent, he became more adamant. She could not break him down. Notwithstanding all her tenacious pursuit of him, he would not yield. And finally, "he hearkened not unto her." He would not even listen.

But it became necessary for him even to go out of hearing. He refused even "to be with her." He kept away from her, out of her sight, out of the house altogether. It is always a helpful thing to do, to put oneself out of the reach of temptation. In Joseph's case it could not be done completely or permanently. He knew, and his master's wife knew, that he must return to the house. His duties made such a return necessary. He was responsible for everything in the house, all its affairs, all its arrangements. His temptress bided her time. She knew it would come.

Long and Searching Thoughts

Meanwhile Joseph indulged in long and searching thoughts. The chief element in the situation that confronted him was not the appeal it made to low and base passion, though that was not negligible. Rather, it was the possibility it presented to throw off his condition of slavery and perhaps assume the station of a man of rank in the world. That did have its appeal, and it was a most powerful one.

He again considered the circumstances surrounding him. It was no scheme of his that had brought about the situation in which he found himself. Moreover, there were things connected with it that made this trial a hard one. There were possibilities in it of enormous importance, possibilities that might contribute much toward the fulfillment of the great promise of his dreams. Then, too, he was away from the restraining influences of home and loved ones. There was no eye of mother, father, or sister upon him, exerting incentives to all that is clean, true, and noble. We little realize what restraints against wickedness and all that is unworthy, low, and ignoble we possess in the expectations of our loved ones for us, and in their confidence in us.

Then, too, Joseph was in a land of heathenism. The moral standards about him were low. Such intrigues as confronted him were common. Others had carried such an act through. So could he. To engage in it would be the customary thing, nothing unusual. We give little thought to the extent we are helped in maintaining virtue by the high ideals and level of conduct we find about us, and also by the certainty that certain lapses of conduct will bring disgrace and the condemnation of society upon us. These social restraints were absent in Joseph's case.

It was on far higher grounds than these, however, that Joseph met the great moral crisis of his life. His answer to the temptation was not on the basis of expediency, of policy, of what others would think of it, of what he could get out of it, or what he might lose by it. The narratives of his father and grandfather had made him acquainted with God. He had come to know God. He had given himself to God, to do His will rather than his own. And so his answer to the great temptation was just this— God!

Two Three-Letter Words

The elements of Joseph's supreme test had come into right focus in his world of thoughts. He could now see them clearly. They had been reduced to their ultimate simplicity. They could be represented and expressed by two three-letter words. On one side was SIN. On the other side was GOD! God was Joseph's answer to temptation.

There is always the answer, the only right answer, the one true answer, the single supremely adequate answer. The tempter came to this slave youth to sweep him away from his true course, and Joseph's answer was—God! The enchantress stands before him, doing her utmost, exerting all her allure, to entice him to impurity. His response was—God! "How . . . can I do this great wickedness, and SIN against GOD?" In such a case a man must get back to his religious principles; he must get back to basic things, to eternal things, to immovable, unshakable things. He must get back to God. It is no good at such a time to cast up what is expedient or inexpedient, or to refer to the example of the other man who has dealt with the same temptation before him. He must get clear away—to God!

From that elevation he must answer the temptation. When he does so from the height of God's throne, he will come off more than conqueror. We are all confronted with temptation. We meet it all the time, everywhere and in every form. It faces us at the turning of every street, at the making of every decision, in the ever-changing maze of daily circumstances. Temptations spring up when we do not look for them, when our guard is down. They come suddenly; they come unexpectedly; they come alluringly; they point us down corridors of flattering possibility. And there is no right, no all-conquering, no adequate, no all-triumphant, answer to the temptations of the great adversary of our souls but Joseph's answer—God! When you fall back on that answer, when you take every

78

temptation to God and meet it in God, then I can assure you that there is no battle you will ever engage in, no storm or flood, no overwhelming temptation, in which you will be without God's protection and power for victory.

Her Final Try

When Joseph could no longer keep out of the house, and again met his master's wife, he found her determined to bring her long pursuit to a decisive and successful conclusion. If persuasion was not sufficient to gain her will, she would be done with persuasion, with words, with verbal enticements, she would use physical contact. She would use her body to break through his reluctance, to overcome his resistance.

She awaited her opportunity. Very likely she *arranged* her opportunity, for the record is that when her time came, "there was none of the men of the house there within." To bring that about in a great establishment would have required some arranging. And when Joseph put in his appearance, with her alone in the house, she renewed her proposal. He appealed to her again to look at the situation as he saw it. His master trusted him, had charged him with the responsibility of his whole establishment, trusted him implicitly. To do what she urged would be to betray that trust; she ought not to urge him to that enormity. And then he added his final, his supreme, argument—"How . . . can I do this great wickedness, and sin against God?"

She did not listen. She cared nothing about unfaithfulness to Potiphar. Breach of trust meant nothing to her. She was indifferent to any "great wickedness." She knew nothing and cared nothing about sin. She was unacquainted with God and had no desire to become acquainted. There were none to see them. They were alone. She threw herself at him. "She caught him by his garment." She attempted to throw her arms about him. "And he left his garment in her hand, and fled, and got him out." Joseph wrenched himself free, letting his cloak fall away from him as she clung to it, and got away from her and away from the house altogether.

She stood there, a frustrated woman, a flouted woman. Her advances had been repulsed. Her victim had eluded her grasp. The glowing light of passion in her eyes died out—to be replaced by the blazing light of hatred and the anticipation of vengeance. Joseph would pay for this.

CHAPTER 14

Imprisonment for Obedience to God

JOSEPH got away from the house and from his temptress as quickly as he could. His mind was bound to be filled with questions about the outcome of the situation into which he had been precipitated. Potiphar was not at home, being occupied elsewhere. When he returned and learned what had taken place, what would he do; what action would he take? But, then, would he learn what *had* taken place? What would he be told? It was not to be expected that Potiphar's wife would expose her shame to her husband. Joseph was sufficiently acquainted with her by this time to realize he could expect her to present the situation to Potiphar in a light that would distort the truth and conceal the real facts. How far she would go in that direction, however, he had no way of knowing. He was filled with such a tumult of thought that he had forgotten his cloak.

Potiphar's wife, however, did not propose to lose any time in setting the stage for her husband's return. Her first move was to arouse the household, to call back the servants whom she had formerly gotten out of the house. She had an act to put on, a part to play. By the time Potiphar returned she wanted the entire personnel of the establishment to be buzzing with the story of the indignity shown her by this Hebrew slave, and the outrage he had attempted on her.

Therefore, fiercely grasping the coat of Joseph, she set herself to screaming as Joseph fled the house. Screaming and calling for help. The servants came running from all quarters, gazing with amazement at their distraught mistress, who stood before them swinging Joseph's coat from side to side while she loudly bewailed the attack she would have them understand had been made on her virtue, and the foul thing this Hebrew slave had done.

"See," she said, as she held forth Joseph's coat, "what has come as a result of your master's bringing in this Hebrew to supervise his affairs and putting him over you. It has gone to his head. He forced himself into my room and attempted to rape me. I screamed so lustily that he was frightened from his dastardly attempt and fled the house. But I grasped his coat as he turned from me, and here it is to witness against him. Potiphar shall be told of this shameful thing, and justice shall be done to this Hebrew wretch."

And with that she dismissed them, knowing that they would magnify everything she had said against Joseph. That was what she wanted. She was indeed suffering from a sense of outrage as she claimed. But the outrage was not to her sense of honor. It was because her amorous advances had been repulsed. And, of all things, by a slave! The more she brooded over it the more determined she became that Joseph should be made to smart for this. "And she laid up his garment by her, until his lord came home."

It must have been a very tense household during the time that everyone waited for the coming of the master. Joseph could not have failed to realize that he was confronted with another major crisis of his life. He could not know what Potiphar would be told. He had no way of knowing what he would do upon being told. He could only wait. But while he waited he had the satisfaction of knowing he had acted honorably. He had not betrayed his master. His motives had been pure. Of these there were two. They are disclosed in his protestation to Potiphar's wife. One was loyalty to Potiphar. His master had trusted him, trusted him with no reserve. He had put everything he had in Joseph's care. Joseph had not betrayed that trust. He had not been guilty of the base wrong to his master to which he had been solicited by his master's wife. There had been no disloyalty on his part to the man who had placed confidence in him. He had not been a traitor to his friend. Regardless of the consequences of offending this woman of high rank, he had not swerved from the path of duty. He had, at least, kept his honor unstained. He felt clean about that.

Joseph's Estimate of Sin

The other motive that had actuated him was loyalty to his God. "How ... can I do this great wickedness," he had said to Potiphar's wife, "and sin against God?" He was glad, now, that he had said that. He had been true to God. He had not yielded to temptation. Confidence grew in him that God would see him through. He reminded himself that the God he served, the God of his fathers, was Jehovah-jireh. He said it over again softly to himself. "He will see to it"; "He will provide."

And we must not pass by this incident in Joseph's career without emphasizing the fact that he was clear-eyed in sensing that the sin to which he had been tempted, and which he had avoided, was not merely a sin against Potiphar, or against Potiphar's wife. It was a sin against God. We should recognize that all sin is against God. It will become more abhorrent to us as we see it thus in its true light. David recognized it when in the time of his penitence he said, "Against thee, thee only, have I sinned." Every act of our life has reference to God. To Joseph, treachery to Potiphar was sin against God. He was right. When we sin against innocence and purity we sin against God. We can never get away from our relation to God in any of our deeds, no matter what they are. Disloyalty to others does not stop there. It is also a sin against God. It will help us immeasurably if we adopt, as our own, Joseph's estimate of sin.

But while Joseph was pleased that he had not been drawn away into treachery against his master, nor into sin against his God, at the same time he was aware that he had made an implacable foe of his master's wife. A great poet has declared that "hell hath no fury like a woman scorned." Joseph could not realize, however, to what lengths Potiphar's wife would go in seeking revenge. She was determined to bring about his utter ruin. So long as he lived she would not feel at ease. She would be satisfied only with his life.

As she looked down upon the garment she had snatched from his shoulders she thought she saw her opportunity for vengeance. By the time Potiphar finally came in she had contrived her story, and she built it around that cloak. Her cunningly woven tale is thus recorded:

"The Hebrew servant, which thou hast brought unto us, came in unto me to mock me: and it came to pass, as I lifted up my voice and cried, that he left his garment with me, and fled out."

Did Potiphar Believe His Wife?

That was a story calculated to rouse a husband to such an outburst of anger that he would slay a slave out of hand. He could do so with impunity, without fear of consequences to himself. Joseph was his property. He could do with him as he willed. The account he had been given, of an attempted assault on his wife, was designed to inflame him with murderous passion and prompt him to give immediate orders for Joseph's execution. It failed of that purpose. Potiphar did not have Joseph put to death. Could it be he did not believe the lurid account his wife had given him?

Potiphar had lived with this woman for years. He knew her character thoroughly. He was aware of her capabilities in the art of deception. His suspicion was aroused that she was seeking retaliation upon his favorite slave for some real or fancied slight. Moreover, he had lived with Joseph for years and believed he knew this Hebrew youth for whom he had developed a real affection. What his wife told him was the complete opposite of what he had come to know about this slave, altogether contrary to every trait of character that he had revealed over the course of ten years of acquaintance. So he knew his wife, and distrusted her. And he knew Joseph, and had every confidence in him.

Consequently, he was able to hold his wrath well under control. However, he had no choice but to make it appear that he believed his wife, and must cover her honor by visiting some form of punishment upon the man she declared had made an attack upon her. But he had no intention of allowing that punishment to take the form of death. His wife's honor must be vindicated. His own injury must be paid for. Joseph's life must be saved. That was the complex situation that confronted Potiphar.

And he took care of it quite satisfactorily. That is, quite satisfactorily to all concerned, with the possible exception of Joseph. And even in Joseph's case imprisonment was to be preferred to loss of life—for imprisonment was the lot that was assigned to Joseph in the settlement that was made.

To the Dungeon

Potiphar's wife was probably not wholly satisfied, for her hatred and malice were such that nothing would have made her content short of Joseph's execution. She could not bear that this slave who had flouted her should live. But she knew she could not crowd Potiphar too far. She was aware of the confidence he had in Joseph, and of the lack of confidence he had in her. She did not want to press the matter to the point where he would demand an investigation. She was already uneasy regarding what Joseph might say to her husband, and she had forebodings that whatever Joseph said would be believed rather than her story. Indeed, she wondered why Joseph had not already sought a hearing and a vindication. Her best course, she decided, was to let the matter rest with Potiphar's decision, in the hope that if she did not further stir it up, Potiphar would let it alone. That was, she felt sure, the better course for her.

Why did Joseph keep silent about the actual facts of what had taken place? Why did he not vindicate himself to his master by telling him what had occurred? There is nothing more trying than to live under false and humiliating accusations. Joseph's character was gravely misrepresented and damaged by the lying report of Potiphar's wife. This would most effectively bar any further advancement he might hope for. It certainly was calculated to retard, if it did not defeat altogether, the realization of his dreams. He had it in his power to set the truth before his master. Why did he hesitate to do so?

Why Was Joseph Silent?

Joseph felt a deep sense of indebtedness to Potiphar for the kindness his master had shown him and for the confidence he had manifested in him. He knew that if he told Potiphar the facts of what had taken place, his master would very likely believe him. He had it on his tongue to put a very different face on the matter than Potiphar's wife had done. But he stopped himself in time. If he should do that he would bring shame and suffering to the one man in Egypt who had shown him kindness, and the one man whose good will he cherished. To tell this man the truth about his wife would bring pain to him. To save this man from hearing the truth Joseph chose rather to suffer the punishment that belonged to his master's wife. To expose her would be to allow the blow to fall on his master's honor.

Rather than utter a word that would hurt Potiphar he preferred ignominy for himself. He would subject himself to cruel suspicion that he had foully wronged the man whom most he should have protected. And he maintained that merciful attitude after his long imprisonment was over and he was elevated to high station. When he had it in his power to punish the woman who had so cruelly wronged him, he did not lift a finger to do so. In this whole affair he not only did not stain his purity of soul, he also showed the highest qualities of mercy. So he uttered no words of condemnation of this evil woman, but quietly endured her malice. He made no effort to entrap anyone else in his own misfortune.

So far as Potiphar was concerned, all that was expected of him as a man vindicating his honor and the honor of his wife was cared for by sending the slave to prison. This he did, but to a prison under his own supervision. It was the king's prison, "a place where the king's prisoners were bound." Literally rendered, the words are "the house of roundness." "The round house where the king's prisoners were bound." Kitto, in his *Daily Bible Illustrations,* volume 1, page 382, describes such a place as "an edifice or portion of the official mansion, mostly subterranean, of which the roof, or vault, rising immediately from the surface of the ground, was round or shaped like an inverted bowl. That it was of this nature may be inferred from its being called, in chapter 4:15, the 'dungeon.'" Kitto adds that "such dungeons are still, under similar circumstances, used in the East, and they have usually an aperture at the top by which some light and air are admitted, and through which the prisoners are let down. They are always upon the premises of the chief of the guard or of the magistrate."

Punished as a Wrongdoer

It was to such a place on his master's own estate that Joseph was taken and let down through the opening at the top, and placed in fetters. And we are told in Psalm 105:18 that they hurt his feet with fetters, and laid him in irons. The report of such harsh treatment was bound to circulate throughout the whole establishment, soothing the wounded sensibilities, and satisfying to a degree the blazing hatred of the mistress of the place, and giving the appearance that Potiphar was visiting his wrath on his slave for insulting his wife. And with this it was Potiphar's hope that the matter would be quickly forgotten, and Joseph's lot made somewhat easier, as the minds of all were turned in the direction of whatever new scandal might arise.

It seemed a bad situation. Joseph had not done wrong, but he was punished as a wrongdoer. It must have been hard for him to understand. He had done what he knew to be right. And he was made to suffer for it. He had preserved his integrity in the face of a great temptation. He had not dealt treacherously with his master, nor betrayed the trust and confidence reposed in him. He had been true and honest. He had not stained his soul with impurity. But he was treated as if the exact opposite were true. Did it really pay to serve Jehovah?

It Could Have Been Worse

Bad as it was, however, it was not as bad as it might have been. It could have been worse. It was bad enough to be in prison and be innocent. It would be worse to be in prison and be guilty. Joseph could still look up to God through the opening in his domelike dungeon and make a silent appeal to Him whom his fathers had served. He could ask God to justify him before men and bring him out of this place.

And this he did. He did not lose his confidence. He did not grow bitter. No doubt for a time he was cast down, bewildered, confused. But he held to his principles. Somehow in the darkness God was at work. This seeming setback was in some way, he would later understand, working out God's plans. Joseph came back at last to his old confidence and consolation. He was in the service of the great God of Abraham, of Isaac, of Jacob—in the service of Jehovah-jireh, the Lord who provides, the Lord who will "see to it." Once again he laid everything in God's hands—and waited.

As his confidence in God returned and he became again his old cheerful self, his demeanor changed from despondency to courage. The change was so marked that even as he had gained the confidence of Potiphar, so now he so impressed his jailer as to bring about a relaxing of the rigors of his confinement, a removal of his chains, and better treatment for himself from all with whom he had to do. Indeed, he became the trusted servant of the warden. The keeper of the prison committed to Joseph the care of all the other prisoners. Again he won his way to leadership.

A Link in a Chain

This incident of Joseph's temptation and imprisonment is given the space it occupies in the Sacred Scriptures not because in itself it is of overwhelming importance. Other men of God have been tempted. Still others have suffered imprisonment unjustly. This is set forth because it formed an essential link in the chain of events that brought Joseph before Pharaoh and made him "ruler over all the land of Egypt."

Joseph must have wondered what purpose was served by the train of circumstances that resulted in such an amount of injustice falling upon him. We are inclined to make the same inquiry. Why was everything so seemingly wrong? The answer is that Joseph had to be in the prison so he would be in the direct line of God's providence. Two important prisoners were to be put into that prison shortly. If Joseph had not been there when they were there, what loss would have resulted.

So the sequence of events and the train of circumstances that seem so cruel, so unjust, so uncalled for, all had purpose in them. They were all a part of the working together of all things for good. They were all necessary for the carrying out of God's plans. Joseph was in the right place in prison. He was there at the right time. Every step in the process was under providential control. And the outcome, as we shall see, was supremely right. God knows what He is doing. He knows how to do it. He does not make mistakes. Every move is a controlled move. And when we place ourselves and keep ourselves in His hand, then only and there only can we be safe and assured. He is the God who "sees to it."

CHAPTER 15

Temptation, Resistance, Victory

THE story of Joseph is told in one of the oldest manuscripts in the world. Thrice a thousand years have passed since it was lived and written. Through these centuries it has been preserved and cherished. It has been passed on from generation to generation as one of the most charming and finest pieces of the literature of the world. It has been embedded in and become an enduring part of a book that has been circulated in a thousand languages in every part of the world. The book is known as the Sacred Scriptures, or Holy Writings. This book is made up of sixty-six sections, or divisions, and Joseph's story is in the very first of these, called the book of Genesis, or the Book of Beginnings.

This book, the Sacred Scriptures, is a book of teaching. But it is more than that. It is a book of illustrations. It is a series of word pictures illustrating its teaching. The teaching is the most valuable teaching in the world. The person who has that teaching, and who heeds it and puts it into practice, is equipped to meet successfully any situation that may meet him from birth to death.

The story of Joseph is more than a fascinating story. Rightly understood, it is a manual for right living. It is as valuable now as it was when it was lived and when it was written. It is a treasure chest of instruction for youth today as it has been through the centuries. And we miss much if we allow our interest in the story to obscure our perception of the meaning it was designed to convey.

Temptations Common to All Youth

The temptations common to youth in Joseph's day are common to youth today. What Joseph faced as a purity problem you face now. All youth face it. There has always been a purity problem connected with youth. There have always been young people who have gone down to bitter defeat and shameful failure before the alluring temptations to unchastity. And there have always been other young people who have won glorious victory over these temptations and come through as did Joseph, unscathed and strong. Joseph's experience furnishes a manual of victory over impurity. In this story the youth of today have an invaluable book of instruction on the way of victory over the downward pull of the flesh, with the most vivid illustrations to accompany it. And the young people of today need such a manual as much as, if not more than, the youth of any former age. They are not different from the young people of all times since men and women have been on the earth. And sins of the flesh are more malignant and powerful than ever before.

Those who know the times in which we live, particularly those who are acquainted with conditions existing in schools and colleges, in homes and places of business, know quite well that young people today have a purity problem of major proportions. Moreover, in some vital aspects it is different from that of other days. At any rate, the problem is here in acute form. It is a problem for which there can be no solution other than the one that God enabled Joseph to find, which God Himself provided and which is God's own solution. It is a solution based on the disclosures that God has made in the Sacred Scriptures and illustrated in the moving story of Joseph.

The Way to Purity

These disclosures are found in specific passages of the Holy Writings. They are addressed to youth. The first is:

"Wherewithal shall a young man cleanse his way?" And the answer immediately follows: "By taking heed thereto according to thy word" (Ps. 119:9).

I would like to assume, and I think I am not wrong in so assuming, that every young person who reads these words is eager to discover the way to live a clean life. You do well to notice that this passage suggests that *you cannot drift into a clean life.* To achieve such a life you must first of all *take heed.* Many things in life may require attention. Nothing requires closer attention than this matter of clean living. Here, nothing can be left to chance or to fuzzy thinking and unsure opinion. Least of all can it be left to our own judgment, feelings, emotions, or impulses.

The verse also teaches that there is a single way of taking heed. That is "according to thy word." This can mean nothing else than that there is in God's Word very positive, very definite teaching on the meaning of a clean life and how it can be lived.

Taking Heed

The second passage is:

"I have written unto you, young men, because ye are strong, and the word of God abideth in you, and ye have overcome the wicked one. Love not the world, neither the things that are in the world. If any man love the world, the love of the Father is not in him. For all that is in the world, the lust of the flesh, and the lust of the eyes, and the pride of life, is not of the Father, but is of the world. And the world passeth away, and the lust thereof: but he that doeth the will of God abideth for ever" (1 John 2:14-17).

This is addressed to young people who are strong and pure because they have taken heed according to God's word, and that word is abiding in them, and consequently they have overcome the great adversary of their souls. Nevertheless, they also need to be warned. They also must "take heed." A great contrast is set before them between the love of God and the love of the world, between doing the will of God and following the lusts of the world. It was because the love of God was foremost in Joseph's heart, because he put the will of God before all else in his life, that he gained the victory over unchastity.

Complete Victory

In this passage the apostle John refers to three things as the sum total of "all that is in the world." He declares these three things to be "the lust of the flesh, and the lust of the eyes, and the pride of life." These are the three forms in which human sin finds expression. They are, consequently, the three great sins of every people on earth and of every human heart—lust, covetousness, pride.

Human desires project themselves into three main areas. There is the desire to enjoy things, the desire to get things, and the desire to do things.

The desire to enjoy things has to do with all the appetites of our bodies, the things that may be enjoyed through our senses.

The desire to get things has to do with the world outside ourselves, the things we can get possession of.

The desire to do things has to do with all we may accomplish to affect that world outside ourselves.

Young people want to have a good time, enjoying the pleasures of life. They want to make money. And they have the ambition to make the most of their lives. All these are wholly right, altogether natural, and quite normal.

But when the desire to enjoy things manifests itself in the use of the bodily appetites in a way that is contrary to the will of God, then it becomes the lust of the flesh.

When the desire to get possession of things, to use money, is gratified in a way that is contrary to the will of God, it becomes the lust of the eye, or covetousness.

When the highest human desire, what is called ambition, the desire to accomplish something, to make the most of our abilities and capacities, leads to a life that does not make God its center, we give it the name of pride, the vainglory of life. It is the pursuit of things that glorify self rather than the things that glorify God.

He Was Against Sin

Calvin Coolidge, onetime President of the United States, was a man of few words. While in the White House he attended church one Sunday unaccompanied by his wife. On his return home from church, Mrs. Coolidge hoped she might obtain from him an account of the sermon. When they sat down at the table for dinner she looked for some comment on the morning service. None was forthcoming. Finally, and in some exasperation, she inquired, "Calvin, was the sermon a good one?"

"Yes."

"Was it a long one?"

"No."

Then, after a pause, "Well, what was the sermon about?"

"Sin."

"Well, what did he say about it?"

"He was against it."

If with the help of God and the lessons of Joseph's experience I can get you to be against sin, this book will not have been written in vain.

Some time ago in a book shop I observed some fine-looking books displayed with a sign that read, "Slightly soiled, and greatly reduced in value." Many a young life gets to be like that—slightly soiled, and greatly reduced in value. Sin does that.

So it is a question big with importance that the psalmist asks, "Wherewithal shall a young man cleanse his way?" Which means, "How can a youth keep the road of life clean and clear and unsullied?" The battle is indeed a fierce one, fiercer today in many ways than it was in Joseph's day. Not alone in the outer world of business and pleasure and society and recreation, but also inwardly, there is a citadel which the enemy of our souls is always assaulting. He never stops. By frontal as well as by flank attacks, with great subtlety, he tries to break down resistance and capture the heart. There are times when he makes unchastity most alluring. He entices into some surrender of principle, some sacrificing of ideals, some lowering of standards. More often the attack is insidious, crafty, clever, subtle. Like the action of a sniper from some hidden cover, or like poison gas, his attack comes secretly, silently—devastating, paralyzing, and vitiating the very air we breathe.

The Way of Victory Found

Joseph found the way of victory. It was not in himself. He found it necessary to look away from himself, to—God. The fact is that *self can never conquer self.* Joseph's way is not only the best way; it is the only way. You are headed for defeat if you take any other way. "How . . . can I do this great wickedness, and sin against *God?"* That was Joseph's way. It was by looking away from himself to God that he gained the victory. That way will bring you victory too.

But the fact should not be overlooked that to depend wholly on God to win our battles for us does not mean that we are relieved from the responsibility of resisting temptation. The scriptural injunction to "submit to God" is immediately followed by "resist the devil." No man has conquered sin apart from any effort of his own. Joseph did not. When he resisted "day by day" he was reinforced, as we are always reinforced, by the direct power of God. As with Joseph, so always that is the sure way to victory.

CHAPTER 16

The Pharaoh's Two Prisoners

THE captain of the king's guard, the royal executioner, committed his slave, Joseph, to the dungeon. But Joseph did not go alone. The record is, "But the Lord was with Joseph, and shewed him mercy, and gave him favour in the sight of the keeper of the prison. And the keeper of the prison committed to Joseph's hand all the prisoners that were in the prison; and whatsoever they did there, he was the doer of it. The keeper of the prison looked not to any thing that was under his hand; because the Lord was with him, and that which he did, the Lord made it to prosper."

The old story repeats itself. As it had been in Potiphar's house, so it is again in the prison of the king. Fidelity, industry, cheerful adaptability, and willingness bring their own reward, and a speedy one. By sheer force of character Joseph came to exercise the duties of governor of the prison rather than remaining just another inmate. The keeper of the prison, accustomed as he was to deal with all kinds of criminals and to appraise the characters of men, quickly discerned that in Joseph he had a different sort of person to deal with from those usually committed to his care. Quite probably, too, he perceived that Potiphar was not as wrathy as might be expected under the circumstances. The keeper may have shrewdly guessed that Joseph, instead of being guilty of wrongdoing, was being made a scapegoat for another. The real object of Potiphar's anger was not Joseph, and it could be that Joseph was put in prison for the sake of appearances, and to shield another.

In any case, Joseph's conduct was such, his countenance and demeanor were so cheerful, and the strength of his confidence in God was so apparent—and he displayed such willingness to entertain and help his fellow prisoners—that no great length of time elapsed before he had won promotion to the oversight of the prisoners and their activities. Everything was placed in his care. His chains were removed; he could move about freely; and he was entrusted with many of the responsibilities usually carried by the keeper of the prison.

Chief Butler, Chief Baker

Meanwhile, events of great importance to Joseph, though he did not know it, were taking place in the great world above him. At the court of Pharaoh some elements of a plot, possibly against the life of the king, had come to light, and before much of an investigation could be made, some of the court officials were hurried off to be held in custody until the matter could be thoroughly examined and those guilty could be identified with certainty.

Two of these officials who fell under suspicion were brought to the prison where Joseph was. They were put in his care.

They are described as Pharaoh's "chief butler" and his "chief baker." These titles, however, are quite inadequate in conveying an idea of the importance and dignity of the offices they filled. The phrases are, when literally rendered, "the chief of the cupbearers" and "the chief of the cooks." The chief of the cupbearers held an office of really unusual importance. The very life of the Pharaoh was in his custody, and such an office was filled only after the most careful examination in order to select a person who was trustworthy. His position, close to the king, gave him the ear of the monarch, and consequently made it possible to exercise some influence with him. Such a position of constant proximity to the royal person was eagerly sought for and was conferred only upon persons in whom the king and his counselors had the utmost confidence. His duty made it necessary to examine every liquid the king was to drink, to taste a portion of it himself to determine that it was not poisoned. His easy access to the king made him a man sought after by interested persons who desired to bring any matter to the royal attention and win the royal favor for their projects. He was, as a consequence, in a most likely position to be entangled in any intrigue or plot that involved those who were part of the official family of the court.

The chief of the royal cooks had a similar post, but in connection with the king's food rather than his drink. He too occupied a position of great responsibility and must possess the confidence of his royal master.

The royal kitchens, together with all culinary arrangements of the palace, were under his supervision.

Joseph's Sympathy

These were the two individuals, or court officers, who, after Joseph had been a year in the dungeon, came to share his imprisonment. No one now knows what they had done or what it was supposed they had done. Conjectures have been made that an attempt had been made to poison the king, and that in the roundup of all who were connected with the supply of his table, these two would, of course, be gathered in. Such a conjecture is given a semblance of accuracy from the extreme punishment that fell upon the chief baker following the investigation that was made. Only an attempt on the monarch's life seems to demand a sentence of such an extreme character.

These new inmates of the prison were noticeably in such a state of suspense and anxiety that they aroused not only the interest but the warm sympathy of Joseph. He could not help seeing their downcast looks, and he marked the uneasiness and foreboding that characterized their demeanor. He sought for ways to lighten the burden of their minds, showing them every kindness and sympathetic consideration.

Joseph could not possibly know what bearing on his own future welfare the coming of these two men would have. It was not with that in mind that he showed them kindness and endeavored to alleviate their gloom. But with their coming a fateful development in Joseph's career had arrived.

The significance of the occurrence is put with deep understanding by the great London preacher Joseph Parker in his comment on Genesis, which is a part of the Peoples' Bible. He writes:

Everything in Life Has a Meaning

"No man liveth unto himself. There is a little upset in the king's house, and, somehow or other, that will be linked with all these events that are happening a little way off. You run against a man in the dark; he remonstrates with you in a vexed tone, and, in that vexed tone, you hear the voice of your own long-lost brother. You go over the street without knowing what you have gone for, and you meet the destiny of your life. A child tells you its little dream, and that dream awakens a blessed memory which throws light upon some dark and frowning place in your life. Some people do not believe in dramas, not knowing that all life is an involved, ever-moving, ever-evolving drama. Life is a composition of forces. The chief butler gives Pharaoh the cup with a fly in it, and the chief baker spoils his baking. These things are to be added to some other things, and out of this combination there is to arise one of the most pathetic and beautiful incidents to be found in all the treasure-house of history. We do not know what is transpiring around us, and how we are to be linked on to collateral processes. There is a main line in our life; there are also little branch lines. You jostle against a man, and get into conversation with him, and learn from him what you would have given gold for, had you known where it was to be found. Everything in life has a meaning. Mistakes have their meanings. Misunderstandings will often lead to the highest harmonies. No man can do without his fellow men. It is a very sad thing, indeed, that we have to be obliged, in any sense, to a butler or a baker. But we cannot help it. It is no good attempting to shake out of the sack the elements we do not like. We cannot colonise ourselves in some fairy-land, where we can have everything according to our pick and choice. The labourer in the streets, the child in the gutter, the poor suffering wretch in the garret,—all these, as well as kings and priests, have to do with the grand up-making and mysterious total of the thing we call human life. God is always coming down to us through unlikely paths, meeting us unexpectedly, causing bushes to flame and become temples of his presence. We go out for our father's asses; we may return crowned men. There are some people who do not like religion because it is so mysterious, not knowing that their own life is a constantly progressing mystery. Whenever they would deliver themselves from the presence of mystery, they must deliver themselves from their very existence."

The arrival of these two notable prisoners meant much to Joseph even before they had their significant dreams. They had moved in court circles. They knew what went on in the country. They were intimate with the great men of the nation; familiar with its statesmen, its courtiers, its military men, its priests and scientists, all of whom frequented the court of Pharaoh. In his daily intercourse with these men Joseph had opened to him opportunity for gaining information of a valuable nature, information that he put to good use when he later joined court circles.

He learned much regarding the character of the king, about the customs and practices of court life, about the influences that swayed public thinking, about the details of government, and the general conditions that prevailed in the nation and among its people. Court officials in disgrace are much more liable to be communicative about affairs of state importance than are court officials enjoying court favor, especially to a person in Joseph's position.

Pharaoh's Birthday

It was customary in connection with the birthdays of the Pharaoh to arrive at decisions regarding the fate of political prisoners—to set at liberty those who were to be freed and to execute those who were to die. It was not surprising, therefore, as this birthday drew near, that the chief butler and chief baker found their anxiety greatly deepened. Three nights before Pharaoh's birthday both of these men had dreams that they believed had something to do with their fate. But review them as they would, they could not arrive at any assurance of their meaning. They both had the impression that their dreams were prophetic.

The next morning when Joseph saw them he found them more than usually pensive, even sad. Knowing something of sadness himself, he expressed his sympathy for his fellow prisoners by inquiring, "Wherefore look ye so sadly to day?"

They responded to his inquiry by replying, "We have dreamed a dream, and there is no interpreter of it."

Joseph knew something about dreams. He was interested at once. He wanted to help these men. Perhaps God would enable him to do so by giving him special understanding regarding the meaning of their dreams. He could not realize how important this moment was to be for him. But now, as always, it was habitual with him to look to God for direction. He was led to say, "Do not interpretations belong to God? tell me them, I pray you."

In saying this he had no thought of claiming to be God, or even of possessing the wisdom of God. He did, however, have the disposition to do what he could to help these men, and he spoke out of a conviction that God would enable him to provide that help by giving him an insight that would make it possible for him to provide meaning to what they had dreamed.

Joseph Had Not Lost Faith

It is plain from Joseph's answer to these troubled men that he had not lost his faith. He still believed in his own dreams. Therefore he still believed in God, notwithstanding his long years of disappointment and deferred hope. After such an experience as his, many a man would have said to these dreamers, "Forget your dreams. Dismiss them from your thoughts. They mean nothing at all, and the less attention you give them, the better for your peace of mind. Dreams are mere delusions. I've had mine, and see where they have gotten me. I once thought, as you do, there might be something prophetic about them. I have learned that this is not true. They are only a mockery to delude you. They did that to me. They will do that to you."

But while that might well have been Joseph's attitude, nevertheless it was not. He had not become bitter. He had not lost hope. He had retained his confidence in God. The obeisant sheaves and the reverential stars still meant something to him, even after all these frustrating years of waiting and of steadily declining fortunes. He did not hold his dreams lightly. He would not, therefore, hold lightly the dreams of these anxious, troubled men. They meant something. He hoped they meant something good, something good to them, perhaps something good to himself. In that faith and with that hope he spoke kindly to these two bewildered and heart-stricken men and offered to become interpreter of their dreams. In doing so, and entirely unconsciously, he took one more step toward the realization of his own dreams.

The Chief Butler's Dream

Joseph's kindness and sympathy warmed the hearts of these men, and they willingly told him their dreams. The chief cupbearer spoke first. He said:

"In my dream, behold, a vine was before me; and in the vine were three branches: and it was as though it budded, and her blossoms shot forth; and the clusters thereof brought forth ripe grapes: and Pharaoh's cup was in my hand: and I took the grapes, and pressed them into Pharaoh's cup, and I gave the cup into Pharaoh's hand" (Gen. 40:9-11).

As the picture unfolded to Joseph with the words of the chief butler, the meaning of the picture was made clear to him. There was no hesitation about his interpretation. He was quite confident as he explained to the chief butler that within three days, on Pharaoh's birthday, the king would restore him to his office. He disclosed his own implicit confidence that this would certainly take place, by adding an appealing statement and making a wistful request. He said to the cupbearer:

"Think on me when it shall be well with thee, and shew kindness, I pray thee, unto me, and make mention of me unto Pharaoh, and bring me out of this house: for indeed I was stolen away out of the land of the Hebrews: and here also have I done nothing that they should put me into the dungeon."

This plaintive appeal makes Joseph altogether human. While he had heretofore refrained from voicing his disappointment at the long years of waiting, at the outrageous misfortunes that had fallen on him one after the other, while he had not allowed his bewilderment and impatience to break forth in wild protests or attempted to make any vindication of himself, nevertheless, it is plain, with this appeal to the chief butler, that he was weary of delay and injustice. "You have good fortune before you," he says. "I wish I could look forward to the same. I would like to be delivered from this dungeon. It is true I have been set over these other prisoners. Nevertheless, I remain a prisoner myself. I am still in bondage, and unjustly so. I am made responsible for the others and placed in charge, but the dungeon is still a dungeon, and I do not belong here. When your good fortune comes, do not forget me. Show me the kindness to do what you can to get me out of here." And the chief butler, elated at the good fortune in prospect, willingly promised to do what Joseph asked.

The Dream of the Chief Baker

The chief cook had listened to the telling of the chief butler's dream. He had listened, too, to Joseph's happy interpretation. And because it was an interpretation with a good outcome, he was encouraged to relate his own dream, hoping for an equally happy outcome. He said:

"I also was in my dream, and, behold, I had three white baskets on my head: and in the uppermost basket there was of all manner of bakemeats for Pharaoh; and the birds did eat them out of the basket upon my head."

Joseph's face must have fallen as the meaning of this dream was disclosed to him, even as the chief baker was relating it. The interpreter for

99

God has always a task of the highest importance, but it is not always a pleasant task. Sometimes it brings heartbreak. He does not always have good news to tell. There are times when it is the announcement of coming doom. It was so in this case. Joseph might search as he would for words to soften the blow he must deal. But he found none. He had to come out with it. And he did not hesitate. "Within three days you will be hanged." How can a thing like that *be* softened?

After all, it was not Joseph's interpretation. It was God's. As Joseph had pointed out, interpretations are with God. Joseph was only spokesman for God. And spokesmen for God must say only what God gives them to say. They must tell of doom as well as salvation. They must speak of God's wrath as well as God's grace. Being spokesman for God is always a high and noble work. It is not always an easy work. It was not easy for Joseph on this occasion. God's interpreters, His spokesmen, cannot always speak words that are pleasant. They are always to speak words that are true. True words are not always pleasant to hear. They were not pleasant to the chief baker. They were, however, true, as the chief baker learned in three days.

So it turned out as Joseph had said. The chief butler was found innocent and restored to his post of duty and honor; the chief baker was found guilty and was hanged. And Joseph was left in the dungeon. The chief butler promptly forgot Joseph, together with his promise to remember him. Time went on, and more years passed over Joseph's head, giving him plenty of time to think the long, long thoughts that came crowding in upon him.

CHAPTER 17

The Forgotten Man

IT WAS a touching and pathetic appeal that Joseph made to the chief butler when he told him of the prospects of his early release from prison, his clearance from all suspicion of disloyalty to the king, and his restoration to his office as chief of the cupbearers. In the upsurge of joyous relief that came to the chief butler he fervently vowed that he would remember Joseph and go to work to obtain his freedom. No doubt he meant it at the time, but in the tumultuous joy that accompanied his vindication and the giddy swirl of events surrounding his restoration to honor and position, all thoughts of Joseph were driven from his mind. He did not even want to think of the dreadful dungeon or anything connected with it. The record is "Yet did not the chief butler remember Joseph, but forgat him."

Let us not blame the chief butler overmuch for forgetting the man in the prison who had shown him kindness and given him hope. It is a very human failing. We would do well, before lashing out at the chief butler, to recall some of our own lapses of memory. It was easy for the cupbearer to allow Joseph to slip out of his world of thoughts. He had been hurried from the dungeon back to the palace of the king, surrounded with all the gala excitement of the king's birthday festivities and the congratulations of his friends and associates, reunited with the members of his own family, decorated once more with the insignia of his position, surrounded by courtiers, and caught up in a swirl of rejoicing and happiness. The dungeon seemed far away, only a bad dream. The chief butler was plunged into all the excitement of this new life, which was still the old life blessedly restored to him. The pleasant greetings of his old associates rang in his ears, and there was the necessity of catching up with all the neglected business that had accumulated during his imprisonment. He felt a high level of gratification at escaping the doom of his colleague, the chief baker, and being transported from the gloom and despair and tormenting uncertainty of his days of detention to his restored position of importance, honor, and intense activity. Considering all this, we can readily understand how the promise he made to that poor Hebrew prisoner was crowded out of his mind.

The Chief Butler Forgets

Quite possibly there may have been an occasion or two when in the midst of his occupations the thought of Joseph came to him and reminded him of his promise. If so, he very likely persuaded himself that he was only waiting for some favorable opening to speak a word in his behalf. He may also have reasoned that, after all, his indebtedness to Joseph was not a great one, for all his fellow prisoner had done was to interpret a dream. He had not in any way contributed to his release. Moreover, there may have been some question in his mind as to whether it would bring him some considerable embarrassment to disclose that he had been on such intimate terms with, or was under any sense of obligation to, a Hebrew slave charged with and in prison for a criminal offense against another court officer.

And so "did not the chief butler remember Joseph, but forgat him." He became absorbed in the activities of the palace, while Joseph languished in the dungeon. While the one was again in the blaze and brilliance of court life, basking once more in the royal favor, the other waited, waited, and waited in the cheerlessness of the dungeon. Day by day hope sprang in Joseph's heart that this might be the day that would bring the release he longed for. As each day closed without any word coming to him, his hope dimmed, and the darkness closed in about him once more. And each day's end saw a deepening of that darkness. The days and weeks and months went by, and there was no word. And finally there was no more expectation that there would be any word. How could hope be sustained in the face of such deadly silence?

It was then that the long, long thoughts came to Joseph. He had spent ten years in slavery, followed by two years in the dungeon. He was now 29 years of age. The years were passing over his head. He had no foreseeable prospect of ever being delivered from prison. One day was following another, and the years of injustice behind him seemed interminable, while the years of continued injustice ahead of him seemed equally endless. His dreams? What had become of his dreams? And God. What had become of God? Had those dreams really meant what he thought? Had he been wrong all along?

Expectations Not Realized

Nothing had come out as he had believed it would. Each development that came to him seemed to make his prospects worse, not better. His expectations had not worked out. The beliefs that he had formed as a result of what his father and grandfather had told him about the dealings and the character of the God of his people all now seemed wrong. At any rate, they had not worked out. The theory he had come to believe to be true, and which his father and grandfather had most certainly taught him, was the one that was accepted as true by all who were servants of the true God—that prosperity and success were always the result of faithfulness in serving God; good would come to those who were good, evil and adversity would come to those who were bad.

It had not been that way with him. It had been exactly the opposite. The more faithfully he had served God, the worse it had been for him. He had certainly tried to be good. He had always been obedient to both his earthly and his heavenly father. He had believed that divine favor would come upon him and he would be rewarded with the blessing of Heaven as a result of his fidelity. He understood that adversity was the mark of divine anger and disapproval. But it was not prosperity that had come to him. It had not been the divine blessing. It had been adversity— not once, not twice, but invariably, year after year after year, for twelve years. How had he benefited as a result of his integrity? What had he gained by his faithfulness to God? Just this—the murderous jealousy and blazing hatred of his own flesh and blood; and slavery; and exile in a strange land. What was the good of being true to God if that was the reward? And that had been his reward.

Moreover, when that beautiful and highly placed Egyptian temptress had thrown herself at him, and appealed to the passions that were at full tide in his young body, had he not, in order to be true to his allegiance to God, resisted her blandishments and her seductive solicitations because he would not sin against God? What had that gotten him? Just this—the stigma of having committed the very thing he had resisted; the punishment for doing the very thing it had been so difficult not to do, and which he had not done. His punishment had been wholly undeserved.

Was There Any Good in Serving God?

And again, he had been kind and considerate to his fellow prisoners. He had listened to their stories. He had tried to comfort them. He had endeavored to bring them good cheer. And what had that gained him? So far as he could see, just nothing. He might as well have kept his kindness to himself. He would have been just as well off. Take those two prisoners from the court. He had gone out of his way to encourage them. He had interpreted their dreams for them. The chief butler had thanked him, thanked him fervently, promised to do all he could to bring about his release from the dungeon. What had it all come to? Just nothing. The chief butler, instead of remembering him, had forgotten him. He had done nothing for him. Enough time had now gone by to make it sure he was not going to do anything. Everything had turned out badly. And from the beginning. And for years. The more he did right, the more he had suffered for it.

What then was the use of being good? Had his father not been mistaken when he taught him that good came to the good, that evil came to the bad? By long experience he had seen that just the opposite was true. The bad prospered; the good were punished. That is the way it had been with him. And he had given it a good trial. Twelve years of it. Had he not better find a more rewarding philosophy to live by? Could it be, after all, that there was no God who judged rightly between good and evil on the earth? Had he been wrong all along? Were Abraham, Isaac, and Jacob also wrong?

Such were some of the thoughts and temptations that must have raced through Joseph's mind after all hope had departed that any good would come to him by the intercession of the chief butler. The days that passed over his head then must have been bleak ones.

As a boy everything about Joseph's training had a tendency to softness. His doting father did everything to spoil him. Joseph reveled in his ornate and princely coat of many colors. He may have allowed the foreshadowed greatness promised by his dreams to exaggerate his importance. His thoughts were turned in overmuch on himself. All of this tends to a lack of real strength, or grip, or power to rule. It would take much to change such a trend that began in youth. But that change was brought about by the long sequence of experiences through which God brought this child of destiny, and by which he became a man of firmness. Joseph had come to the great opportunity of his life. And he was ready.

His elementary schooling had been given in the tents by means of the teaching contained in the narratives of his father and grandfather.

His secondary, or high school, training had been obtained in the house of Potiphar during the years of his slavery.

His college work, now nearing graduation, had been gotten in the dungeon, where he had been assigned altogether unjustly.

His life lessons had been thoroughly learned. He had been a diligent and obedient student. And his Headmaster from the beginning, as well as his chief and constant Teacher, had been and still was the God of his fathers, Jehovah-jireh, He will "see to it." The record is that "he [Joseph] was there in the prison. But the Lord was with Joseph."

Yes, the Lord was with him. He had been with him always. In his father's tent, on the journey to Dothan, in the pit, on the journey to Egypt, on the slave block, in Potiphar's house, in his temptation, in the dungeon, the Lord had never forsaken him. Even in this disappointment caused by the forgetfulness of the chief butler, the Lord was with Joseph.

God Uses Even Ungrateful Forgetfulness

For it would not have been good for Joseph if the chief butler had been successful in gaining his deliverance from imprisonment. That would have been harmful, not helpful. It was a good thing for Joseph that the cupbearer forgot him. God can use even ungrateful forgetfulness for the furtherance of His own plans, even as He used the hatred and malice and injustice of Joseph's brothers.

Consider for a moment what would have happened if the chief butler had remembered Joseph, and set himself to overcome his natural reluctance to intercede for this Hebrew prisoner. Suppose he had done so and had been successful in getting him out of the dungeon. What then would have been the outcome? He was still Potiphar's slave, but he never could have been restored to Potiphar's house. He could have been put once more on the slave block and sold to another master, possibly to work in the quarries or some other place of toil.

But suppose Pharaoh's good will should go so far as to restore his liberty altogether and allow him to depart from Egypt to his own country and people. Such an outcome would have been welcome, and would have brought a time of great joy to Jacob and happiness to Joseph. But, after all, it would have meant only a return to sheeptending, to sheepshearing, to cattle-dealing, to watching and checkmating his brothers' plots. It would not take him in the direction of the fulfillment of his dreams, but rather to some obscure ending of his career.

In that case, when the years of great plenty came there would have been no Joseph in Egypt to store up grain against the coming years of famine and want. Egypt would not have had a foreseeing food administrator who would know that lean years were coming and needed to be prepared for. When the great famine came, there would have been no Joseph in Egypt to save that nation and feed other nations round about. When the famine struck at the very life of Jacob's family, there would have been no Joseph in Egypt from whom to obtain sustenance to preserve life. There would have been no Joseph in Egypt to provide a safe place for his people, that they might grow into a great nation. No, it was best for Joseph that the chief butler forget him, and that he remain a while longer under the discipline of the dungeon. Granted it was hard, but it did not really hurt Joseph.

Hard but Profitable Years

Two years passed by after the chief butler had been set free and restored to his post in the palace of the king. They were the finishing years of Joseph's education and preparation. They did much for him. His active mind, thrown in upon itself, again went over the basic principles of his early training, the fundamentals of his religious faith. Notwithstanding the forbidding nature of his surroundings and the seemingly hopeless condition that showed no prospect of a change, he was enabled to put God first in his thoughts, and God's will first in his expectations. It must, indeed, have been trying beyond words to see the chief butler obtain the speedy fulfillment of his dream while he who had made known the meaning of that dream, he who had waited so long, was left waiting still. Even more trying must it have been to be left so completely unbefriended by the departure of the chief butler that there seemed no possible way of again connecting himself with the great world outside the dungeon walls.

Hard years, indeed. Nevertheless, they were most fruitful years in maturing Joseph's character. The self-possessed dignity, the impressive confidence, the firm assurance of knowing God's will, and the ready ease of command that he displayed when he was so unexpectedly and suddenly precipitated into Pharaoh's presence had their roots in these two years of silence and waiting. Joseph was forced to find some basic principle that would sustain and carry him through this time of waiting, that would direct his course in the midst of disappointment and deep perplexity. He found that principle in the conviction that had been growing with him through the years—and which now became fixed and settled regardless of the prevailing darkness—that the one essential thing to be fostered and accomplished in this world was the doing of God's will and the carrying out of God's purpose. Let God's will be done, whether known or unknown, let God's purpose go on, whether seen and understood or hidden and not understood, and all else that should go on will go on.

Furthermore, Joseph came to the firm belief that the man who best fulfills God's purpose and carries out God's will is he who, without anxiety or impatience, simply waits on God's time and does the plain duty of each passing hour. Without knowing what God's purpose was for himself, or God's time for carrying it out, he came to learn the supreme lesson of leaving all that, too, in God's capable hands, and accepting for himself a profound and willing and active submission to the all-knowing will of the Eternal. He was, after these years of intense training, fully in tune with the Infinite.

God has large use for a man so trained and so governed. And as Joseph was now ready to be used, God was likewise ready to use him. Joseph's time of training was over. Joseph's great hour had come.

CHAPTER 18

From Dothan's Pit to the Lordship of Egypt

THE great changes and events in the life of Joseph had a way of happening with startling swiftness. They happened that way now.

For years he had been the favorite of his father, shielded, petted, secure. All at once, without warning, he was menaced with death and plunged into a pit.

Suddenly he was separated from his home and his father's love and protection, and sold into slavery—transported to Egypt and put upon the slave block.

Achieving a degree of security and importance in Potiphar's household, and finally being placed in charge of this whole establishment, he found himself suddenly immured in a dungeon with clanking chains and fetters on his feet.

And now from that condition, after years of waiting, he is just as swiftly, by the remarkable providence of God, exalted to the government of the first nation on earth.

When things did happen to Joseph they happened with unexpected suddenness, and with changes of an astonishing extent.

Three years he had been in the dungeon. His imprisonment was wholly undeserved. No means of redress were within his reach. His cause had never been fairly tried. There was no prospect it would be fairly tried. There was no way by which his innocence could be established. From every human viewpoint his case was beyond hope.

God Never at a Loss

What now happened to Joseph should impress upon us a lesson that we would do well always to keep in mind. It is that there is no situation, no matter how desperate, from which God cannot speedily deliver us.

There is no state or condition into which men or devils may precipitate us that takes us beyond the reach of our heavenly Father. Do not allow any combination of circumstances, no matter how complicated and seemingly impossible, to cause you to believe that God has lost His ability to help you, to bring you deliverance, to change your hopeless captivity into glorious victory. When God's time has come He can make every difficulty vanish. He can cause every barrier to disappear. Nothing, literally *nothing*, can stand in the way of the carrying out of His purpose, the fulfillment of His will. And God's intervention to completely change the circumstances of a life can come instantly.

It does not matter that you see no way out from a completely hopeless condition. God can see what you cannot see. You may be in, or be brought into, great trials that present what seem to be insurmountable difficulties. They may be caused by the loss of some loved one, by some embarrassing circumstances, or by some other calamitous events. You may come to think your situation is hopeless, and be unable to perceive any way of escape.

If and when such a time comes to you, do not lose your confidence in the God with whom nothing is impossible, even though every human help has failed you. Never is His arm shortened that it cannot save. Never is His ear heavy so that it cannot hear. Your extremity may easily be His opportunity. He is never at a loss for means by which to effect His gracious purposes.

Joseph Was Ready

It was God's will and purpose that Joseph, the Hebrew slave who was the inmate of a dungeon, should be elevated to a position of the highest dignity and power in the land of Egypt. He had decreed this in order that His future purpose for His people should be carried out. He now proceeded to carry out His decree, to put His purpose into effect. The time had at last come, the time fixed in the eternal purposes of God, for the revelation of what God had in mind for Joseph.

There had been no premonition to Joseph to herald the approach of his deliverance and his elevation. The events that now occurred with breath-taking rapidity took him entirely unawares. Nevertheless, they did not find him unprepared. He was ready.

While Joseph slumbered in the dungeon, things were taking place in the great world above his head, over in the palace of the Pharaoh, that were to prove of enormous significance. The king had a dream. A relatively insignificant thing. Nevertheless, it made an enormous stir in the affairs of Egypt. It was no ordinary dream. As a matter of fact, it was a double dream. It was the way God took of disclosing to this king some things about the future that he should know, that he might be a true father to his people.

Pharaoh's Dreams

In his dream the king was standing by the river. Up out of the river came seven fat cows that began feeding in the meadow. As he watched, seven thin, lean, famished cows came out of the river, and they ate up the fat, well-fed cows. After they devoured them they remained as lean as before. Then the king in his dream saw seven wonderfully good, full, bursting ears of corn, followed by seven wretched, withered ears of corn. The poor thin ears of corn proceeded at once to devour the full and fat ears of corn. But even so, they remained as thin and withered as before.

That was what the king saw in his dream. It entirely ruined his rest for the night. He was troubled. He had a distinct impression that his dreams had something to do with the welfare of his kingdom. He had a second impression that these dreams had a divine origin. A great anxiety came to him. His fears were aroused. He felt a sense of excitement moving within him. He could not interpret the dreams. He did not know what they meant. He was sure, however, they meant something of supreme importance. And he knew he could not rest until he learned their meaning. It was with the utmost anxiety that he waited for the morning, when he could summon his counselors and discover someone who could disclose to him the meaning of these tantalizing dreams.

The morning came. With it came the summons that went out in all directions for the counselors of the king to hasten to the court and attend at once upon the king. The great city awoke as its avenues filled with hurrying chariots bearing the leading men of the nation to the palace. It became obvious to everybody that great matters of state were on foot. The courtiers, the higher ranks of society, were alerted and also began to hasten to the court. A general movement of the people began a convergence upon the vicinity of the palace. A widespread curiosity developed into an increasing excitement as the throngs of people clamored for information concerning the cause and meaning of the developments going forward.

The Counselors Assemble

The counselors were brought in before the king. They assembled with grave and sober countenances on which were plainly written the sense of concern and anxiety that by this time had spread widely. They listened intently as the king explained why he had called them together, and with such haste. He made it plain that he was deeply convinced that this matter concerned the welfare of the whole nation. He then related what he had dreamed.

It turned out that not one of the king's counselors could throw the faintest ray of light on the meaning of the dreams. They were all at a loss. It can be readily understood that this would make the monarch's anxiety the greater. As he gazed about upon the bewildered faces of the men who were his trusted counselors, and realized that not one of them could unlock this secret for him, his feeling of uneasiness became so overwhelming that he knew he could not again have peace of mind until this perplexing development was made clear.

Together they decided to summon others outside their number—students of the occult sciences, priests, magicians, learned men of science, the wise men of the nation, the scholars, men who had employed their time in the examination of just such mysteries. And so the messengers went out to gather together the best minds of all Egypt. Again there was a hurrying through the streets of many chariots bearing the learned men of Egypt to the king's aid.

These too listened to the king's narrative of his dreams. Not a man among them was of any help. They were all equally dumfounded. The king was distracted. His agitation spread among his associates and courtiers. Enough information came out of the counsel chamber for the people thronging the palace and the adjoining streets to gain some idea of the situation. Among those who learned of it was the chief butler, the forgetful man. Two years before, he had had just such a painful and anxious experience himself. It all came rushing back to his mind. The similarity of the case of himself and his colleague, the chief baker, struck him forcibly. Instantly he thought of that young Hebrew who had so accurately and with such ease interpreted their dreams. He recalled how exactly the events fulfilled the interpretation. It came to him that of all the men in the kingdom, he might have it in his power to solve the king's problem. Immediately he sought to find a way to have himself brought before the king. In this he succeeded.

Joseph Hastily Summoned

He told the king and the assembled counselors his story. He did it most adroitly. He moved most lightly over the embarrassing fact that he had been in prison at all, and the circumstances that had sent him there. But he made it plain that while there he had met a most remarkable man who was astonishingly gifted in the matter of dream interpretation, that this man, a Hebrew by nationality, had foretold for him, and with great particularity, the meaning of his dream and that of the chief baker, and that this interpretation had been carried out with exact precision in even the smallest detail. What the interpreter had declared would come to pass was the thing in each case that *had* come to pass.

He finished his account and refrained from making any suggestion, contenting himself with telling his simple story. He did not presume to advise that Joseph be sent for. It was possible that Joseph might not measure up so brilliantly in this case as in his own. If that should happen, it would serve his interests better not to have given any advice. But the effect of his story was exactly as he thought it would be. The king hurried off a messenger to the dungeon. He was impatient, as were the counselors, for the appearance of the man about whom they had heard such a remarkable story.

And so the clatter of a racing chariot penetrated to the interior of the dungeon, awaking in every inmate's heart the swift hope that the summons might be for himself. The excitement at the palace became the excitement in the dungeon. Who was to be called? The messenger of the king came in. The man Joseph was summoned and must hasten to the king. The record is that "they brought him hastily out of the dungeon." The margin here has "They made him run," which conveys some idea of the intensity of the excitement that prevailed everywhere.

But they did not make him run so speedily that he was thrown off balance. That he maintained his equanimity and self-control in spite of the turmoil all about is evident from the fact that "he shaved himself, and changed his raiment" before he "came in unto Pharaoh." The prevailing excitement did not stampede Joseph. He kept his head. The king, impatient as he was, would have to wait until the proprieties were cared for.

Among other things that Joseph had learned in his association with the officers of the Pharaoh was that court etiquette demanded perfect cleanliness and propriety of dress. In the minds of Egyptians these were of such importance that otherwise important matters could be postponed until these were in order. So Joseph, after three years in the dungeon, could calmly refuse to be hurried even by an imperative summons of the king, until he had shaved himself and obtained and donned suitable clothing. In every sense of the word, when Joseph's great hour came he was ready.

It must have been a thrilling experience for Joseph, just out of the dungeon, to step into the palace and look down the endless corridors flanked by statuary and pillars, with the most luxurious of furnishings, and ornaments of precious metals and stones. He must have gazed with wondering eyes upon the assembled nobility of the earth's greatest nation as he was hurried into the audience chamber of the king.

The King Explains

Wonderment was not his alone, however. It was with similar wonder that the king and his courtiers and counselors looked upon this handsome, self-possessed man, now thirty years of age, who stood before them clean shaven, properly accoutered, waiting with quiet courtesy to be told the reason the king had need of him.

The king's explanation was most simple and came directly to the point. "I have dreamed a dream," he said, "and there is none that can interpret it: and I have heard say of thee, that thou canst understand a dream to interpret it."

It is an impressive and beautiful thing, and a revelation of Joseph's real character, to notice how at the very outset he put God forward in this first interview with Pharaoh and his first appearance before the ruling class of Egypt, even in the presence of the high priests of Egypt's idolatrous religion. To the statement of the king that he had been summoned because the king understood that he possessed exceptional ability to understand and to interpret dreams, he modestly replied, "It is not in me," and immediately added that God was the source of any proficiency he might have in that direction, and that he was confident that "God shall give Pharaoh an answer of peace."

With that comforting assurance, Pharaoh at once proceeded to relate for Joseph's information the details of his dreams. When he had completed the telling, there came from Joseph an immediate explanation. And it directed attention again first of all to the true God. In the midst of this throng of influential and high-placed idolaters at the court of Egypt, Joseph was not ashamed to speak of and for his God. "God," he said, "hath shewed Pharaoh what he is about to do."

Joseph Interprets

The seven good kine, he went on, stood for seven years. The seven good ears of grain were likewise seven years. The seven ill-favored kine were seven years. The seven withered ears of grain were likewise seven years. The meaning of the dream was simply this: There were about to come in Egypt seven years of bountiful harvests of great plenty, of unusual prosperity. These were to be followed by seven years of extreme famine, so extreme that the previous years of abundance would be blotted out and forgotten, famine and want so widespread and desperate that they "shall consume the land."

The reason that the dream was "doubled unto Pharaoh twice" was "because the thing is established," that is, certain, bound to take place. Moreover, "God will shortly bring it to pass."

Because the developments foretold in the dreams were right upon them, Joseph presumed, on the basis of what was about to come to pass and the urgency of the matter, to add to his interpretation a word of counsel. Let Pharaoh, he said, make haste to "look out a man discreet and wise, and set him over the land of Egypt." He then proceeded to outline a plan of national food conservation for the gathering and storage of enormous quantities of produce during the seven years of abundance, in order that this surplus food might be available against the years of extreme need that were to follow. He also outlined a national plan of food administration and general welfare for the famine years, "that the land perish not through the famine."

All this left the king and his ministers of state and heads of department quite a full agenda to work on. Having been given, however, an astonishingly comprehensive blueprint of the best thing to do for the welfare of the nation by this amazingly sagacious young interpreter, who gave the impression of speaking for God and with the wisdom of God, they quickly reached their important decisions, which the king took it upon himself to announce. What Joseph had recommended "was good in the eyes of Pharaoh, and in the eyes of all his servants." It is doubtful whether such unanimity had been exhibited in the counsels of state in Egypt for a long time on any other matter respecting the national welfare.

Joseph Elevated to Second Place

Pharaoh said, "Can we find such a one as this is, a man in whom the Spirit of God is?" No one presuming to call that in question, the king turned to Joseph and said, "Forasmuch as God hath shewed thee all this, there is none so discreet and wise as thou art: thou shalt be over my house, and according unto thy word shall all my people be ruled: only in the throne will I be greater than thou." "See, I have set thee over all the land of Egypt. . . . I am Pharaoh, and without thee shall no man lift up his hand or foot in all the land of Egypt."

Breath-taking, indeed! In the dungeon in the morning; in the palace by night! A condemned slave when the day began; the lord of all Egypt at the day's end. At sunrise wakening to another day of hope deferred; at sunset looking back on a day of blazing glory, release, and fulfillment of the cherished hopes of years!

Joseph must have had a difficult time composing his mind to rest that night. He was in the palace of the king. He was invested with the powers of the king. The highest honors in the gift of the earth's greatest nation had been conferred on him.

God Would "See to It"

And as you would expect in the case of Joseph, with his God-centered life and with such a training as he had experienced, his thoughts did not settle on his glory or his great honors—but upon Jehovah, the God of his fathers, who had brought it all to pass. He was supremely the God who would "see to it." And how wondrously He had seen to it.

Joseph's mind must also have turned to his dreams. He had been occupied during the day with Pharaoh's dreams. But now he could think of his own. They forecast some great service—service to his God, service to his family, service to God's cause in the earth, service that would help forward God's great purposes. He would be on the alert for that. His brothers' sheaves bowing down to his. The sun, the moon, the eleven stars making obeisance. God was not through with him yet. What had taken place today was a beginning, not the ending. It was a part, not the whole. This was only commencement. But what a commencement! And so Joseph went to sleep.

Potiphar! He must have been in that throng of the king's counselors and courtiers. This was certainly one occasion when the captain of the royal guard would not be absent. Had Joseph recognized him? Had Potiphar cause to be uneasy about what Joseph would say to the king or do to him?

And Potiphar's wife when she learned of the day's developments! Dear me, what a buzzing of excited talk there must have been in Egypt's great houses that night while a tired and exiled boy from Canaan enjoyed his rest!

CHAPTER 19

The Divine Timetable

LET us catch our breath after looking on at the developments of the story that has been unfolding before us. As we pause, let us make sure that in our absorption with the main features of this remarkable history we do not miss some other things that are an essential part of it, but which may remain in obscurity unless special attention is focused upon them.

We have been looking on at a series of wonderful providences. The thrilling interest of the details of the story may blind us to lessons they teach; but these lessons, if well learned, are bound to be of enormous value. I would turn your attention now, and have you consider well, how God has managed every development in Joseph's experience in such a way as to carry forward the great design that has been in the divine mind from the outset. I do not want you to miss seeing that while the purposes of God were slowly maturing in the great world outside Joseph's range of vision, Joseph's character was similarly ripening during these years of slavery and imprisonment into the strength and self-discipline that would fashion him into the instrument fit to carry out what God had in mind. God is always shaping men and women, by experiences He allows to come to them, into tools fit for His use.

God's Wonderful Over-all Supervision

Let your mind once again run over the outstanding occurrences of Joseph's story. His brothers cast him into the pit. Their action and the hatred that inspired it were wicked. But it did not hurt Joseph. God can use even the hatred and malice of men and turn it to good. His brothers sold him into slavery, a most evil thing. But God used it to move Joseph into the place where he could be trained for great service.

The foul lie that Potiphar's adulterous wife told about Joseph precipitated him into the dungeon. It was an iniquitous miscarriage of justice. God's controlling hand, however, used those hard circumstances to place Joseph where he would receive a training and perfect a character that would fit him for future service of great value.

The ingratitude of the chief butler in his forgetfulness and neglect were wholly inexcusable. They left Joseph suffering in the dungeon during a period, and it seemed an interminable period, of painful waiting. But God used the waiting to further prepare His chosen instrument for the use He had for him, and to keep him close at hand against the time when he would be needed for a work of stupendous importance.

So we are enabled to see in it the wonderful over-all supervision of God. Every link of the chain is fitted into its own place with most delicate and timely precision. No development comes a moment too soon. Not one is allowed to lag and arrive too late. The providences of God are like the nature of God. There are no haphazard movements in His works. The great orbs in space—sun, moon, stars, planets—move with exact precision. Their transits, circuits, eclipses, and conjunctions can be and are calculated a thousand years ahead and known to the minutest fraction of a second. Never does the sun rise too late. Never does a star set too early. All movements are under divine control. In the providential arrangements presided over by God for all His works, everything has its fixed time. And the clock of God is always right—never a second slow, never a second fast.

Chance Plays No Part

Chance has no part in it. One writer has put it in the words "It chanced! The Eternal God that chance did guide." Can the perfect adjustments displayed all about us in the functioning of nature and all its activities be merely chance? Look at the marvelous beauty and timeliness of providence. Can it be possible that these are a mere endless succession of fortunate coincidences? That would be incredible. There is a God in heaven. He made the complex machinery of the universe. His hand governs that machinery and controls its activity. That God is our heavenly Father. At the center of the universe a heart beats. That heart is a heart of love. And He has ordained that "all things work together for good to them that love God."

118

So there was a providential control in Joseph's life and affairs, as there is also in yours. With perfect and precise adaptation every smallest event in Joseph's experience was exactly timed and worked into the final result. The callous and inhuman wickedness of his brothers in selling him into slavery, the despicable lie of Potiphar's wife that sent him to the dungeon, the ingratitude and indifference of the chief butler that abandoned him to a lengthening of his imprisonment—all these injustices and wrongs from others were under the divine control and were, by the divine and benevolent hand of God, turned into blessings.

Do You Recognize God's Providence?

It is not difficult for us now, as we look back on the story of Joseph, to recognize God's providences in his life. But are we to suppose that the life of this shepherd lad was in the hand of God in a way that is not true of us? Is there in our lives less of God's providential supervision than there was in the life of Joseph? At the time he passed through his experiences Joseph may not have recognized, indeed he did not recognize, the hand of God. Later on he saw that God had controlled everything that happened to him from the beginning. When he made himself known to his brethren he relieved their fears by saying, "I am Joseph your brother, whom ye sold into Egypt. Now therefore be not grieved, nor angry with yourselves, that ye sold me hither: for God did send me before you to preserve life. . . . God sent me before you to preserve you a posterity in the earth, and to save your lives by a great deliverance. So now it was not you that sent me hither, but God." And on a later occasion Joseph said to his brothers, "As for you, ye thought evil against me; but God meant it unto good, to bring to pass, as it is this day, to save much people alive."

So it is with us. The hard blows that are dealt us in the circumstances that surround us now and the trying experiences that test our characters are not seen at the moment to be what they really are. As with Joseph, so with us; it is not until afterward that we see our disappointments, hardships, trials, misfortunes, as well as the wicked things done to us by others and designed by them to harm us, to be parts of God's providential supervision of our lives. It is only in retrospect that we see them as instruments to carry forward God's purpose in our lives. We will surely come to see this if we firmly and faithfully seek to carry out the will of God, and if we keep ourselves from marring His plan by taking our lives out of His hands. Keep in mind always that God is never hurried; the perfecting of character He has in mind is a slow work.

We have looked at Joseph's life and experiences in what we may designate as the hard years. From now on we shall be looking at him in experiences that seem to have in them nothing but brightness and prosperity. Before turning from the old to the new we will be helped if we take time to consider some things the story of Joseph should impress upon us.

It is rather the usual thing for men, both young and old, to consider that when hard and trying experiences come they must have done something that has displeased God, something wrong, and that He has sent these afflictions upon them to manifest His displeasure and punish their delinquencies. This is not necessarily so. There are trials that the all-wise God and Father allows to come to His disciples for purposes of testing and of character development, as well as trials that may have a punitive purpose. Many times we distress ourselves needlessly by imagining that the God we serve could never have permitted such evil things to happen to us, or to our loved ones, except to punish us for something wrong we have done.

Such a philosophy is a mistaken one. There are trials that are tests, not punishments. They are trials of faith, of patience, of fortitude, not rods to scourge us for being particularly wicked. God's people are tried, tested, trained, developed, shaped for the work into which at length He will fit them. He has told us that "whom the Lord loveth he chasteneth." Trials, then, are not always an evidence of God's displeasure; they may be the evidence of His love and care.

Hardships Can Be Blessings

Hardships may be a blessing. They were to Joseph. But the blessing is not in the hardship; it is in the way it is met and borne. Bear it impatiently, and with grumbling and murmuring against your lot, and the trial will be a curse, not a blessing; and you will be the worse for it when you might have been the better. The suffering that was designed to enrich us, borne impatiently, will impoverish us. But if we learn to endure our trials with patience, as being permitted by a loving Father as messengers from Him to teach us things we cannot be taught otherwise, then His hand upon us will be precious, and what God has to say to us by His afflicting agents will have music in their messages and bring comfort that will revive and cheer our hearts.

We do well, too, to bear in mind that God is never lacking in ways and means to turn our captivity into deliverance. We may see no way of escape from the hard conditions that oppress us, but God's discernment is not thus limited. Because we see no way out we are prone to think such a way does not exist, that our state is hopeless. We should learn to lift our eyes from conditions that to us are quite impossible, and fix them upon our God, with whom nothing is impossible. Human help may not be able to reach us; He can always reach us.

From our reading of the record of His dealings with men, and from our observation of His providential working in the affairs of men and in our own personal affairs, we should understand and believe that it is always in God's power to bring to pass His purposes regardless of all opposing circumstances. The most unlikely and unlooked-for events may be made—have been made—to serve His gracious designs and to accomplish what human foresight could never have effected.

Help Must Be Found in God Alone

It should also be pointed out that as in Joseph's case the servants of God are never in a fairer way to deliverance and happiness than when they are patiently waiting on God and subjecting themselves to His will. Everything connected with Joseph discloses that he was fully resigned to the will of God, quite ready to wait for God to act. It is true that he had at the time of the release of the chief butler allowed himself to form some expectation from the arm of flesh. Two ensuing years of human ingratitude, however, had convinced him that his help must be found in God alone. Taking his eyes from man and fixing them wholly upon God quickly resulted in the bestowal of his recompense and ample compensation for all he had suffered. He puts off his prison garments, and with them his sorrows. From his state of oppression and humiliation he is made the benefactor and the savior of a whole nation.

Our most favorable course is to leave ourselves in God's capable hands and look to Him alone to "see to it," submitting ourselves in all things to His wise and knowing disposal. The sooner we learn to say "Thy will, not mine, be done," the sooner we are likely to be favored with the desires of our heart. It is a great lesson to learn, and a most rewarding one. It takes a lot of learning. But when we bring ourselves with cheerfulness to submit to every dispensation of God, we will learn as Joseph did that no matter how long trials have accumulated in our experience, God can and will bring them out to our advantage. No matter how great or how long-continued they may be, the outcome, either in this world or the next, will leave us with no cause for complaint.

Joseph's Reward

Joseph had left himself in the hands of God. He had patiently awaited God's time. He now has his reward. In a single bound he rises from the dungeon and stops only at the foot of the throne. The contempt of his brothers had been exchanged for the eager reception of the proudest court in the world. The hands hardened by the toil of slavery are adorned with the signet ring of the king. The fetters on his feet are exchanged for the chain of gold a monarch has put around his neck. The princely garment of a doting father and the robe left in the hands of the adulteress are replaced by the garments of fine linen from a royal wardrobe. He was despised and trampled on by his oppressors, but now all Egypt is commanded to bow in his presence as he rides forth in the second chariot, chief minister of Egypt, second only to the king. What a far distance it is from the sheepfolds of Hebron and the goatskin tents of his father!

There is a light shining from this moving tale of long ago that should shine into many a life today, bringing with it rays of cheer and hope for those who may be waiting on God in the midst of disheartening circumstances. The dear heart of a heavenly Father is beating in the life experience of each of His disciples. The hand of an all-wise God is working out for each one of His children the predestined outcome of a divine plan. The hour for full revealing may not have struck on the great clock of God. But it will strike, never doubt. Your times are in His benevolent hand. Just learn this, friend of God: For the glory of God, and for your own good, your Father in heaven bids you lay down your burden of anxiety. Trust all to Him. He has guided unnumbered millions already through life. He can, He will, lead you. All things even now are working together for your good. Turn the helm of your life over to the hands of the Captain of your salvation.

THE DIVINE TIMETABLE

Let me bring this chapter to a close by inviting your attention to a singularly illuminating and wonderfully helpful comment on this early phase of Joseph's experience made by Ellen G. White in her remarkable book *Patriarchs and Prophets,* pages 222, 223:

"How was Joseph enabled to make such a record of firmness of character, uprightness and wisdom?—In his early years he had consulted duty rather than inclination; and the integrity, the simple trust, the noble nature, of the youth bore fruit in the deeds of the man. A pure and simple life had favored the vigorous development of both physical and intellectual powers. Communion with God through His works, and the contemplation of the grand truths intrusted to the inheritors of faith, had elevated and ennobled his spiritual nature, broadening and strengthening the mind as no other study could do. Faithful attention to duty in every station, from the lowliest to the most exalted, had been training every power for its highest service. He who lives in accordance with the Creator's will is securing to himself the truest and noblest development of character. 'The fear of the Lord, that is wisdom; and to depart from evil is understanding.'

"There are few who realize the influence of the little things of life upon the development of character. Nothing with which we have to do is really small. The varied circumstances that we meet day by day are designed to test our faithfulness, and to qualify us for greater trusts. By adherence to principle in the transactions of ordinary life, the mind becomes accustomed to hold the claims of duty above those of pleasure and inclination. Minds thus disciplined are not wavering between right and wrong, like the reed trembling in the wind; they are loyal to duty because they have trained themselves to habits of fidelity and truth. By faithfulness in that which is least, they acquire strength to be faithful in greater matters.

"An upright character is of greater worth than the gold of Ophir. Without it none can rise to an honorable eminence. But character is not inherited. It cannot be bought. Moral excellence and fine mental qualities are not the result of accident. The most precious gifts are of no value unless they are improved. The formation of a noble character is the work of a life-time, and must be the result of diligent and persevering effort. God gives opportunities; success depends upon the use made of them."

CHAPTER 20

The Food Administrator

THE record is that "Joseph was thirty years old when he stood before Pharaoh king of Egypt." It had been a long road he had traveled since leaving his father's dwelling place thirteen years earlier, when at his father's request, he had set out to search for his brothers to inquire into their well-being, that he might bring his father word again. Much had happened during those thirteen years, and all of it had had a bearing on bringing him to the place where he now stood—at the foot of the throne.

The trials that had come to him had not been easy to bear—but every one of them had played its part in moving him closer to his present hour. The fiery temptation he had resisted, the foul lie of his temptress, the unjust imprisonment, and the interpretation of his fellow prisoners' dreams—all these had been necessary to bring him before Pharaoh, and they were written into the record to make plain to us how it was that Joseph came to be introduced to Pharaoh and the court life of Egypt. His willingness to become the interpreter of the dreams of other men, even when he had no obligation to help them, brought him to the place where he was enabled to make an important contribution to the long-delayed fulfillment of his own dreams.

With great suddenness he is summoned to become God's interpreter to Pharaoh. He does so with an impressive dignity and convincing positiveness. In doing so he displayed such wisdom in reading the meaning of Pharaoh's visions that he created the profound conviction, not alone in the mind of the king but among his courtiers and counselors as well, that he was the man, and the only man, who could successfully carry out the comprehensive plan that he had been led to suggest for saving the nation.

THE FOOD ADMINISTRATOR

More Than He Had Expected

Joseph could not have dreamed, when he proposed to Pharaoh that he seek out a man to set over the important business of administering the nationwide project of storing up and distributing the surplus food of the seven years of plenty, that he would be the man selected. His dreams did not carry him that far. He was a Hebrew, an alien. Moreover, he was a slave. Worse, he was a prisoner, cleaned up and allowed liberty only for the occasion. His most ambitious imaginings could not bring him to think it to be within the limits of possibility that Pharaoh would pass by all these tried officers and ministers of state who crowded around him, and settle upon an inexperienced youth from a dungeon, one wholly untried, of a different race, a different religion, under a cloud of criminality. To do so might prove deeply obnoxious to the populace and most offensive to his counselors.

Quite possibly Joseph may have had hopes, and might even have expected, to win sufficient friendship and good will from Pharaoh to result in his deliverance from the dungeon, even possibly to obtain some subordinate position in which he might hopefully begin life anew. It is altogether unlikely, however, that his hopes reached beyond that in the crowded moments during which he stood before the monarch, outlining what God would shortly bring to pass and making his sagacious suggestions as to how best to meet the great crisis that would shortly confront the nation.

His Sole Thought Was of God

As he stood in the royal presence the only allusion he made to himself was of a depreciatory nature. It was not in him to interpret the king's dreams. That belonged to God. He did not recommend himself to the king's notice or describe any fitness he might have for the post he outlined, or for any other post. He directed the attention of this court to God, not to himself. He might have used the occasion to bring to the king's notice, now that he had disclosed the meaning of the king's dreams, that he had been sold into slavery by his own brothers, that Potiphar's wife, by an atrocious lie, had had him sent to the dungeon (doubtless one was listening who feared this). He might have made a plea for his freedom. He did none of this. His sole thought was to exalt God, not to advance his own interests.

Like Daniel on later but similar occasions, he said, "Let thy gifts be to thyself, and give thy rewards to another." "As for me, this secret is not revealed to me for any wisdom that I have more than any living, but for their sakes that shall make known the interpretation to the king, and that thou know the thoughts of thy heart." "He that revealeth secrets maketh known to thee what shall come to pass."

A Man Completely Devoted to God

The king, the ministers of state, the courtiers thronging the great audience chamber, all together recognized that there was something particularly noble and worthy of admiration in this young man who thus stood there quite alone and nevertheless maintained the fullest allegiance to his God, wholly without ostentation, but with a quiet dignity and naturalness that disclosed that he possessed a great store of strength. The impression he made was of one completely devoted to the interests of the God he served, not to his own. There was that about him which led all who heard him to believe that God was with him, that he was a God-sent man.

With little or no hesitation Pharaoh and his advisers reached that conclusion, and apparently with unanimity. They agreed that to no man could they more safely entrust their country in preparation for the forthcoming emergency they all now firmly accepted as being the certain meaning of the king's dreams and as being sure to come. It seems astonishing that these experienced advisers of the king could have been influenced to do more for this man than make some compensation for his imprisonment, restore his freedom, perhaps confer on him a generous reward. Something induced them to go far beyond this and put in his hands the national welfare itself, making him the head of the state, second only to the king, exalting him to rank and prestige and power far above their own. It is plain that they were profoundly impressed with Joseph, indeed supernaturally impressed. Through him they felt God. This man who had come out of nowhere, miraculously appearing before them in their desperate emergency, had been sent, they felt sure, not only to enlighten and warn them but to save them. They would put him where he could work cut that salvation. Joseph had been self-abnegating to such a degree, keeping himself wholly out of sight, making himself such a transparent medium, that in his presence these statesmen and great men of Egypt felt themselves to be in the very presence of God.

Lord of All Egypt

This is what moved the court of Pharaoh and the king himself. Inspiration declares of Pharaoh on this occasion: "He made him lord of his house, and ruler of all his substance: to bind his princes at his pleasure; and teach his senators wisdom" (Ps. 105:21, 22). In the presence of his entire court the monarch with great conviction declared, "Forasmuch as God hath shewed thee all this, there is none so discreet and wise as thou art." The king thus revealed that he believed the supreme God had chosen Joseph to deal with this matter because he was wise in heart.

Pharaoh proceeded without delay to confer upon Joseph all the honors of his new position. He was clothed with a robe of state. A heavy gold necklace marking him as second to Pharaoh was placed around his neck. Pharaoh placed his own ring on his finger, thus transferring his own authority to him. He presented him to the entire court to receive the acclamation of courtiers and people, thus receiving their acknowledgment that he was now the superior of all the dignitaries, princes, statesmen, and potentates of Egypt.

As far as was possible, Joseph was naturalized as an Egyptian. He was given an Egyptian name, easier of pronunciation, perhaps, to the Egyptians than his own, though certainly not to us—Zaphnath-paaneah, which may have been only an official title. Its meaning has been given different explanations. Some understand it to mean "Revealer of secrets." Others interpret it as "Governor of the abode of him who lives" and "Governor of the district of the place of life." The king carried his liberality further by providing Joseph with an Egyptian wife, Asenath, daughter of Potipherah, high priest of On, or Heliopolis. Thus Joseph became connected with one of the most influential families of the nation, and was accepted into the loftiest caste of Egypt, the priestly caste.

Absolute Authority

That the authority conferred upon Joseph by the king was absolute there was no doubt. In Pharaoh's own words, "Without thee shall no man lift up his hand or foot in all the land of Egypt." His first and immediate responsibility was to prepare for the impending famine. To do this he assumed among his other duties that of food administrator of Egypt. His policy was simply to economize during the seven years of extraordinary abundance to such an extent that adequate provision could be made against the seven years of severe famine that were to follow. His plan was that one fifth of the produce of the flourishing years, stored up year by year, would be sufficient to supply the people's needs in the famine years. This fifth was purchased in the king's name from the growers, and was no doubt bought at the cheap rates that would prevail in a time of abundance.

To take care of the surplus of the bountiful years Joseph caused a chain of enormous storehouses to be built. The construction of these buildings began with the first of the years of plenty. Adequate arrangements were made in these great buildings, which were scattered in the important centers of the nation, for preserving the surplus grains of each year's harvest. That policy was maintained without letup throughout the full seven years of abundance. When the years of plenty came to an end, the amount of grain that had accumulated and been stored was enormous. "Joseph gathered corn [grain] as the sand of the sea, very much, until he left numbering; for it was without number."

Family Life

During the busy years of getting ready for the famine Joseph established himself in family life. To him and Asenath were born two sons. He gave them both Hebrew names. We may perceive something of the feelings that influenced his life when we look at the significance of the names he gave these boys. The first-born he called Manasseh, which means "forgetting." His reasoning was that "God . . . hath made me forget all my toil, and all my father's house." It must not be understood from this that he had stopped thinking of his boyhood home at Hebron, or that he would ever stop thinking of it, and with deep affection. How could he? It was there he had learned the things that had shaped his whole life—acquired the religious convictions that had governed his conduct, and that he had never abandoned, and gained the ideals and standards that had molded his character. No, he had forgotten neither his father's home nor his father. All his afterlife is a demonstration of that.

128

What is meant here is based on the same principle underlying the words of Jesus in the New Testament: "If any man come to me, and hate not his father, and mother, . . . he cannot be my disciple." Moreover, it parallels the words of the suitor who in Psalm 45:10 is represented as saying to her whom he desired as his wife, "Hearken, O daughter, and consider, and incline thine ear; forget also thine own people, and thy father's house." It is the language of hyperbole. Everything in Joseph's subsequent history—particularly his solicitous inquiries after his father's well-being when his brothers came to buy food, his tearful reception of the old father when he came into Egypt, the tender care he gave him in the land of Goshen, and his dying request that his bones might be carried back to Canaan—all are definite indications of how lovingly he cared for his father and cherished the thought of his boyhood home.

What he meant by the words used in giving Manasseh his name was that for the first time since he had been sold into slavery he now had a home of his own, a family of his own, a son of his own, and these were the center of his life, and they made up for and reconciled him to the absence from his own people.

To his second son he gave the name of Ephraim, meaning "fruitful." "God," he said, "hath caused me to be fruitful in the land of my affliction." Egypt would never be anything else to Joseph than "the land of my affliction." It would never take the place of Canaan. But in Egypt, nevertheless, God had made him fruitful. He did not fail to recognize, even in his prosperity, that all he had, all his blessings, came from the God he delighted to serve. God "hath made me forget all my toil"; "God hath caused me to be fruitful." God had sustained him all along in his adversity; God had kept him from despair, in the pit and in the dungeon; God had kept him going when the way was hard; and now God is still with him in his prosperity, which God had also brought about, preserving him from pride when, second only to the Pharaoh, clothed with great power and elevated to high place, he rejoices over the little ones in his home. In all the experiences of Joseph and in all his character, nothing stands out with more striking clarity than his faith in God, his life centered in God. And that did not change with changing circumstances. Both in adversity and in prosperity, God was the very center of his life.

Abundance Ends

The seven years of abundant harvests at last came to an end. The storehouses of Egypt were overflowing with surplus grain. Joseph was thirty-seven years old, head of a nation, head of a family. And then "the seven years of dearth began to come, according as Joseph had said." And that dearth was not limited to Egypt alone. "The dearth was in all lands." It spread to adjacent kingdoms and peoples. Indeed, "the famine was over all the face of the earth."

With the coming of the famine years came also God's time to begin the fulfillment of Joseph's dreams. Joseph had been in Egypt, exiled from his home, for more than twenty years. He was ready now for God to use him to the full. And God was ready to put into effect the plans He had in mind when He took him from his father's tent and sent him into Egypt.

CHAPTER 21

Joseph's Brothers Arrive in Egypt

THE famine that raged in Egypt affected as well the land of
Canaan. It became particularly bad in the region where Jacob and
his sons had their encampment. They began to feel the effects of it with
increasing severity. Caravans coming back from Egypt brought the information that Egypt had grain, indeed, had quantities of grain that
could be obtained for a price. More and more caravans passed near the
camp of Jacob, some going to Egypt in the hope of supplying themselves
from her surplus, others returning laden with grain for their people.
Jacob's sons manifested a pronounced reluctance to follow the practice
that seemed to influence all the tribes and families about them.

The news that grain was available in Egypt disturbed the encampment of Jacob. If grain could have been obtained anywhere else, even
much farther away than Egypt, there would have been no hesitation
among Jacob's sons about going and fetching it. But Egypt! They had
no liking for Egypt. They did not want to go to Egypt. They had no
desire to have any dealings with Egypt. Egypt, they felt, was decidedly
out of bounds for them. A long time ago, twenty years and more, they
had sold their younger brother to a caravan whose destination was
Egypt. They had not forgotten. It had rested on their consciences ever
since. Try as they would, the memory would not erase itself. Egypt to
them meant Joseph. They needed grain. They were going to have to
get grain. But the very thought of Egypt made them uneasy.

Conscience Made Them Cowards

Not that they expected to come across Joseph in Egypt. Joseph,
they felt sure, was a slave, if he still lived. Quite likely Joseph was
dead. Slaves did not enjoy long lives. Joseph in the flesh would not

131

bother them. But the thought of Joseph, and of what they had done to Joseph, did bother them. Their consciences for more than twenty years had never ceased troubling them about Joseph. And they feared their consciences would be more active in Egypt than in any other place. They most pointedly and positively did not care to go to Egypt—for grain or for any other purpose.

Jacob had never learned what had happened to Joseph. His other sons hoped he never would learn. Jacob thought Joseph dead. He did not know he had been carried to Egypt. To Jacob, Egypt meant grain. To his sons, Egypt meant Joseph. They were pronouncedly allergic to Egypt. Others could go to Egypt for grain. Not they. If they could manage to hold out a little longer, the famine might pass, and with it the necessity to have any dealings with Egypt. They would like that.

Since the elevation of Joseph in Egypt, during all the seven years of the abundant harvest, of his marriage, of the beginning of his family life, and of the great dignity that had come to him as second only to Pharaoh, he had made no effort to get in touch with his father, to notify him that he was alive, or to visit him. There can be no question but that he could have done so if he had thought it best. It would have been easy for the chief executive officer of Egypt, in charge of the nation's affairs, to have dispatched a messenger or a whole mission to Canaan to bring his father word of his well-being and his exaltation. He could have gone home himself and been his own messenger. He did not do so. He did not go. He did not send.

Joseph Not Unfilial

The seeming neglect to communicate with his father has troubled many readers of his story. It appears to have been a grave defect in his otherwise admirable conduct, a fault in an otherwise blameless character. During the years of his slavery and his imprisonment there had been no way open for such communication. He had been effectually cut off from his old home. But all barriers preventing communication had been removed by his elevation to power and authority. And yet he had made no move to get in touch with Jacob or his old home.

This was no unfilial conduct, as some have supposed. It was not the result of any lack of love. Joseph had learned to wait on God. He did not initiate an important project until God directed him. He had learned to distrust his own impulses. He wanted to send word to his old father, who for two decades had been without any such word. He was eager for his father to know of his exalted dignity in Egypt, as is made evident on a later occasion.

But something stopped him. God's guidance, which had become most real to Joseph, did not point in that direction. Joseph wanted to send word. But it was made plain to him that God did not want him to send word—yet. God had His own time—and it had not yet come. He would have Joseph wait for His time.

And Joseph waited, eager as he was to act. It pays great dividends to be in tune with the Infinite. What a wonderful story, what a wonderful providence, would have been spoiled if Joseph had followed his own natural impulses! God was leading up to the fulfillment of all Joseph's cherished desires in His own way. Not one was to be denied. His way was supremely best. Joseph realized all his desires at last, but in God's way, and at God's time. And that is always the best way and the best time, as Joseph came to learn. And so Joseph left himself in God's hands, kept himself under God's control, submitted himself to God's management, believing that Jehovah-jireh, the God he worshiped, would "see to it."

It is a great lesson to learn—the most valuable lesson in life—waiting in patient submission to the precious, foreseeing, all-wise, benevolent will of God.

Jacob Stirs His Sons to Action

Jacob observed the uneasiness of his sons. He found it hard to understand. Other tribes were sending to Egypt for grain. His own sons, stalwart, active, energetic men, accustomed to provide for all the needs of their families, their flocks, and their homes, hesitated, and seemed helpless in the face of this emergency. The pinch of the famine was growing more severe. Certainly some steps must soon be taken to relieve it. And his sons did nothing.

Finally Jacob called a family conference. There would be no further delay allowed. The situation demanded action, immediate action. He made it plain that the information had reached him that there was grain available in Egypt. Their encampment, all their families, needed and must have grain. Why did they hesitate? They could get grain as others were doing in Egypt. What was stopping them? And then he broke out upon them: "Why do ye look one upon another?"

Jacob had nothing in mind but to stir them into action. He did not dream what the real reason was for their apparent timidity and reluctance. He was thinking of grain. Their consciences were tormenting them about Joseph.

Grain in Egypt

Jacob had to shame them into going. "Why do ye look one upon another?" Was their father growing suspicious? Did he know something? Had he penetrated their guilty secret? If so—well, Egypt after all might be preferable to home. Their father was an old man. During recent years he had visibly failed. He manifested a growing weakness. This was evidence not merely of the slowly passing years but of sorrow. Jacob bore in his heart the scars of many blows, the chief of which was the loss of his beloved Joseph. His steps had grown less vigorous. He pathetically speaks of his "gray hairs." He carried a grief that did not lessen with the years—a grief he had to carry alone. Step by step he went down toward the end of life mourning for his son. Nothing could blot from his memory the sight of the blood-spattered robe, the only relic now remaining of the dear face and form of the one he thought nevermore to see.

"Why do ye look one upon another? . . . I have heard that there is corn in Egypt: get you down thither, and buy for us from thence; that we may live, and not die." In the face of all the circumstances and of that positive order the brothers had no choice. "Get you down thither." Otherwise we face death. And so "Joseph's ten brethren went down to buy corn in Egypt."

The time had come when God meant to use these men to fulfill His own great purposes. He designed to found a nation with them. As He had prepared Joseph by long training to be a fit instrument to fulfill His will, so now He would prepare Joseph's brothers to carry out His purposes. They could not dream of the amazing spiritual experiences that awaited them in Egypt. God tormented their consciences to open their hearts for His gracious guidance and to bring them under the powerful working of His Spirit to transform their natures. They were being prepared for their meeting with Joseph, and the great changes in their own lives that would transform their characters. They were destined to become different men than those who sold their brother into slavery.

Benjamin Did Not Go

It should be noticed that it was his *ten* sons that Jacob sent into Egypt. He did not trust Benjamin to the care of the others. Benjamin at this time was a child no longer. He must have been between twenty and thirty years of age. But something made Jacob hesitate and draw back from sending the only remaining son of his beloved Rachel into Egypt. It has been surmised that Jacob had never been without a lingering suspicion that Joseph had met with some foul play at the hands of his brothers. I do not know. The record is silent here. In any case it is clear that since Joseph had disappeared, Benjamin had succeeded to his place in his father's affections. And Jacob decided against putting his youngest son in the power of his brothers. Benjamin would remain at home.

So the ten brothers, with their beasts of burden and their attendants, set out without Benjamin on their way to Egypt. Whether they discussed Joseph on the way, or exchanged remarks about their mutual uneasiness and forebodings of conscience, we are not told. But that they all thought of Joseph there can be no question. He was much in their minds. They did not expect to see him. That seemed outside the limits of possibility. Nevertheless, they would narrowly watch every gang of slaves manacled at work in the fields or sweltering in the brickyards, preparing material for the pyramids.

On inquiring where they should go to purchase grain they were directed to Joseph's headquarters. While he did not himself attend to the business of selling grain to the people of Egypt, it appears that all applicants from other lands had to submit to the routine of a personal examination for purposes of security. Joseph took charge of such examination of foreigners himself.

A Man of Rank

They were ushered into the presence of this man of rank. They were told he was lord of all Egypt. He was seated as usual at his customary post, surrounded by all the confusion and noise of any Eastern market. All at once his attention was struck by the entrance of a group of ten men, who obviously were strangers and ill at ease. For a moment he gazed at them, his heart throbbing wildly. One good look was all he needed. The record says succinctly, "He knew them."

Oh, yes, he knew them. He knew what sort of men they had been. He wondered whether there had been any change in them, whether they were still the same sort of men he had known them to be. He knew they had come for grain. That made him know that the pinch of famine had reached Canaan—and Jacob. His heart leaped at the expectation that after twenty-two years he was about to learn something of his father.

They did not know him. How could they? From a lad of seventeen he had grown to a man approaching forty. He was clothed in pure white linen, ornaments of gold indicating his rank, a dress perhaps not altogether dissimilar to the princely coat in which they had seen him some twenty-two years before. They were bearded men, roughly clothed, with the stains of travel upon them. He was clean-shaven as was customary with high-caste and highly placed Egyptians. He was the governor of the land.

They Make Obeisance

And in wholly unconscious fulfillment of the dreams of long ago they bowed down themselves before Joseph with their faces to the earth. It is not difficult for us to imagine the thrill that tingled through Joseph as he looked down upon their prostrate forms and recalled his dreams. He must have felt very close to the God who had given the dreams and who at long last had brought about their fulfillment. It was one of the supreme moments of his life.

How little these ten men realized that they were doing anything to fulfill their brother's dreams. They did not recall their mocking and malicious words of the long ago—"Behold, this dreamer cometh. . . . Let us slay him, and cast him into some pit, and we will say, Some evil beast hath devoured him: and we shall see what will become of his dreams"! They were approaching the time when they were indeed about to see what would become of his dreams. But what they would see was to be very different from that which they had planned.

Before we look in on the reception that Joseph gave his brothers, and leaving them low in their obeisance before him, I would direct your attention to certain supremely important things in connection with this long-anticipated moment in Joseph's life. Every participant in this life drama is seen working in his own character, and governing his conduct and actions by his own unfettered will. No coercion is applied to the free agency of any one of them. Notwithstanding, in some inscrutable way, they all combine to carry forward one great purpose. All that they do is made to work together to carry out a single overruling design.

So it has been in all history. So it is now. God has been in history from the beginning—personal history as well as national. That should not be in the least degree incredible or surprising. God is really in the life of each one. It would be deplorable for us to miss the basic teaching of this story by failing to recognize that fact.

CHAPTER 22

Joseph Treats His Brothers Roughly

As HIS brothers stood in his presence after prostrating themselves before him, Joseph's keen eye ran from one to the other in a swift analysis. He wanted first to learn whether his brother Benjamin was with them. He wanted next to appraise these men. He had not seen them for more than a score of years. Were they the same men he knew them to be at that time or were they changed men? His ultimate attitude toward them would be determined upon the answer to that question.

His present attitude has been looked upon as unnecessarily cruel and uncalled for, but Joseph knew exactly what he was doing and he proceeded in the best way calculated to achieve what he had in mind. He had neither heart nor disposition to be harsh or cruel. He wanted information. He set about getting it in a way that would bring out what was in the hearts of these men.

Benjamin, he saw, was not with them. Was it possible that these men had disposed of their younger brother in some way similar to that in which they had endeavored to dispose of him? Was Benjamin dead, or possibly sold into slavery? And his old father; what had become of him? Did he still live? Was he well? Joseph must know. And these men before him—what sort of men were they now? He did not need to inquire what sort of men they were twenty years before. That he knew. What he needed now was to learn whether there had been any change in them.

What Sort of Men?

The appearance in Egypt of Joseph's brothers was quite unexpected by him. Since their arrival before him for investigation on security grounds he had had no opportunity to formulate any plans with reference

138

to them. When they came at a later time on their second visit he was far better prepared with the proposals he thought best to make. Now he was not prepared at all. He did not know whether he wanted these men near him in Egypt. He had no knowledge of them, what sort of men they were, what was their state of mind.

This was the reason he proceeded so cautiously with them, why he made himself strange, why he disguised himself and used an interpreter as if he could not understand them, why he adopted so circuitous a way of arriving at his objective. He wanted an insight into the state of their mind. He wanted to learn whether they were the men he had known them to be. He wanted to discover whether it would be safe to ask them, and be pleasant to have them, to come and live near him in Egypt. And about all these things he must be sure. The course he took to discover all this was about the only course open to him, and at the same time it was the best course to compel them to look into the recesses of their own hearts.

Were They Repentant?

Prison would be about the best place for them to do a bit of contemplative consultation of their own souls. It had worked that way with him. He would try it on them. There was no revenge in this, no vindictiveness. He did not feel vengeful. His most profound desire was to help these men. He felt compassionate toward them. But one great question remained in his mind. Were they worthy of help? This must be determined.

He had one great advantage over them as they stood before him, and he decided to use it to the full to test their characters. He knew them; they did not know him. What he would finally do with them would depend on the results of his investigation. He wanted now to know whether they had experienced anything like regret or repentance for their harsh and brutal treatment of him. For this purpose he continued to disguise his identity while demanding that they disclose theirs. He decided to act a part before them, or toward them, that might recall their sin to them. He decided to treat them in a way calculated to remind them of their treatment of him. From the result he would be able to arrive at a conclusion regarding their characters, which would help him to a decision regarding his disposal of them.

They had excused their cruelty to him, years before, by claiming that he was a spy sent after them to pry into their conduct and report their evil deeds to their father. Very well, that is where he would begin. He inquired where they came from and what their mission was in Egypt. They replied that they came from Canaan and their purpose in coming was to buy food. He asked them for identification.

"Ye Are Spies!"

Then out of a clear sky he broke off his inquiries and abruptly and most sternly accused them of having come to Egypt not on a peaceful errand but a hostile one. They were in Egypt, he declared, to spy out its defenseless condition on its northeast border, and to take back such a report as would induce the Canaanites to launch an invasion at the very time when the whole energies of Egypt were concerned with the privations of its people.

"Ye are spies," he stormed; "to see the nakedness of the land ye are come."

Most indignantly and quite honestly they repelled this charge, more than a little startled that it had been made. Here was something they had not expected. "Nay, my lord," they said, "but to buy food are thy servants come." And to give that credence they added: "We are all one man's sons; we are true men, thy servants are no spies."

It was a good answer, and with an officer who was not acting a part no doubt it would have been sufficient. It made plain that their mission was one of family necessity, not of national ambition.

That, however, was not enough for the investigator who examined them. He had not learned what he was after. He threw it back into their teeth. "Nay," he said, brusquely, "but to see the nakedness [defenselessness] of the land ye are come."

Twenty years and more before, he had made the same protestations of his own innocence when he was in their hands, and they had refused to listen. Now he refused to listen. So they proceeded to produce additional evidence.

"Thy servants," they said, "are twelve brethren, the sons of one man in the land of Canaan; and, behold, the youngest is this day with our father, and one is not." That was more like it. Joseph was getting what he wanted now. Benjamin was alive, free, and at home. Jacob still lived.

140

There was a great surge of relief in Joseph's heart. He was getting results. But not enough. He still needed to know what sort of men these were. He would carry on. Before doing so, however, he was suddenly struck with some statements in what they had just said.

They Thought Joseph Dead

"One is not," they had said. Then they thought him dead! That must have brought a lump to his throat. They had said it with gentleness, as though it brought a tinge of sorrow with it. And, oh, that other expression, "Thy servants are twelve brethren." As he thought of it he was gripped with emotion. Could it be that in that dear encampment of his father, his home, they still thought of the family as unbroken, even though he had been given up for dead? He still belonged, notwithstanding all that had happened; he still had a place in their thoughts, in their hearts. He was one of them. "Thy servants are twelve," not eleven, "brethren."

To cover his emotion, to conceal the upsurge of tenderness that was likely to undo him, he burst out with exaggerated emphasis, "That is it that I spake unto you, saying, Ye are spies!" That is, it is just as I said; you are spies. And I will find a way to try you out and prove it.

"Hereby," he said, with assumed sternness, "ye shall be proved: By the life of Pharaoh ye shall not go forth hence, except your youngest brother come hither." To prove their contention that they were all of one family, he would allow one of their number to return to Canaan for the purpose of bringing back Benjamin. Meanwhile, the remaining nine would be imprisoned until Benjamin's arrival. And all this "that your words may be proved, whether there be any truth in you: or else by the life of Pharaoh surely ye are spies."

With that, and with great abruptness, he closed the interview and ordered them off to prison, that they might weigh their situation and consider whether they would agree to his terms.

They had cast him into the pit. Now the tables are turned. He puts them into prison. Man can cover a lot of sober thinking in prison, and these men had a lot of that kind of thinking to do. Moreover, while Joseph calmly awaited the result, they did it.

He left them in prison three days. Then he summoned them before him. He professed to have relented—that is, to some degree. Their story was still to be tested. But he had thought of their families and of the old man, their father, if such there were. And he considered it more just and merciful to let nine of them return to Canaan, carrying provisions, rather than one. He would retain one as a hostage to assure the return of the nine with their younger brother. In that way their truthfulness and loyalty could be demonstrated, and the charge of spying could be canceled.

And as the reason for his change of plan, he submitted that he also feared God, meaning, apparently, that he did not want to have any injustice burdening his conscience.

That went over their heads for the moment, but came back to them later. They could not think of anything else but the proposal he had made that nine of them could go home with grain. They were eager to accept this. It was much better than for nine to remain in prison while one went home. That was still hard enough, but before he had a chance to make any further changes, they agreed to do as he said.

And now a decision had to be made regarding the one to be selected to remain in Egypt as the hostage. They gathered in a close group to determine that distressing choice. In low voices they consulted together, not overly careful about being overheard by the governor. They were sure he could not understand them in any case. It was then that they spoke out to one another about the meaning of the trouble they were facing. It was a punishment, they felt sure, for what they had done to their brother Joseph long ago. They had treated Joseph roughly, charged him with being a spy, put him into the pit, sold him to the Midianite traders, lied to their father about him. You can readily understand Joseph's interest as he overheard them say, "We are verily guilty concerning our brother, in that we saw the anguish of his soul, when he besought us, and we would not hear; therefore is this distress come upon us."

They Recall Their Sin

Joseph's purpose was being realized. As these men faced the possibility of the same isolation and deprivation of liberty to which they had subjected Joseph, there came to their remembrance their sin against him, and they were impelled to speak to one another about it and to attribute their present calamity to the fact that it was a retribution for their wrongdoing. They recalled how they had refused Joseph mercy when he pleaded with them, and therefore they now need expect no mercy in their own extremity.

One voice among them, however, refused to join in the chorus of confession. Reuben said, "Spake I not unto you, saying, Do not sin against the child; and ye would not hear? therefore, behold, also his blood is required."

They had no suspicion that every word they said was heard by the governor. He was hard put to conceal his emotion as he listened, and to prevent his tears from falling. He was compelled to leave them to themselves for a little time, while he fought back his tears. He was not yet ready to disclose his identity to them. There was more he needed to know. He wanted to learn how they treated Benjamin. To obtain further information, he felt it necessary to continue his disguise. However, he took out of their hands the selection of the hostage to remain in prison while the nine took grain to Canaan. He took Simeon and bound him before their eyes and gave orders that he should be returned to the prison.

Why Simeon? Perhaps because he knew of Simeon's unusual harshness of disposition as displayed at Shechem. Possibly, too, Simeon may have been foremost among the brothers in their brutal conduct toward him.

Having done this, Joseph commanded his servants in the storehouses to fill the sacks of his brothers with all the grain they would hold, together with smaller containers filled with provisions for their journey, and to put in each man's sack the money he had paid for the grain. He then hurried them off on their journey to Hebron.

CHAPTER 23

Full Sacks and Money Back

THE nine men, Joseph's brothers, set out on their return journey to Canaan with uneasy thoughts. Simeon was in prison. To get him released was going to require the consent of their father to allow Benjamin to return to Egypt with them. They doubted that Jacob could be brought to give his consent to such a proposal. They did not look forward with much eagerness to their arrival at the home encampment.

Having completed their first day of the journey to Canaan, they came to a halt at the first resting place. One of them had occasion to open his sack of grain. It was not the small traveling sack but the larger one, which ordinarily would not have been opened until the journey was ended. He was surprised to find resting on top of the grain his bag of money. This discovery was immediately called to the attention of all the brothers, and it added much to the disturbed state of mind of the whole company. They were greatly perturbed, fearing that they had been made the victims of some sort of conspiracy that boded ill for them when the time came for them to return to Egypt. They said, "What is this that God hath done unto us?" Their thought was that somehow this was something added to their retribution, and they would be made to answer for it and perhaps be charged with theft. At least they saw Providence at work in their affairs. God had seen their sins, had marked their conduct, and they feared He was now punishing their wrongdoing.

Their Return to Hebron

Their return to Hebron was awaited with anxiety by their father. They had been gone longer than he had reckoned. When they arrived the whole encampment became a beehive of activity. The occupants of all the tents, the members of every family, gathered about them as they stopped before Jacob's tent. They listened with eagerness as they began the narrative of everything that had befallen them. As Jacob was told of the unfriendly attitude and harsh conduct of the Egyptian governor a feeling of alarm spread among them. It seemed portentous of some evil design on his part. These fears were confirmed when the men came to open their sacks of grain. In each their money was found.

And when Jacob came to learn of what had been done to Simeon, he could contain himself no longer. His deep distress burst forth in the doleful words, "Me have ye bereaved of my children: Joseph is not, and Simeon is not, and ye will take Benjamin away: all these things are against me."

It was a very bitter outburst, and a very inaccurate one. Here was an old man who did not know what he was talking about. For the entire statement, from beginning to end, contained not one single fact. It was wholly a mistake. So far as Jacob knew, it was all true. But Jacob did not know. He was not bereaved of his children. Joseph was not dead. Simeon was not lost to him. And while they would take Benjamin away, they would also bring him back. Nor were any of these things against him. On the contrary, they were all for him. They would all come out to his benefit. They were all working together for his good, not for his harm.

How prone we all are to be influenced by first appearances, to arrive at hasty conclusions, and pronounce judgments upon incomplete processes. Poor Jacob! Very likely he would smile in later years as he thought of his words. But it was very real to him at the time. It is not to be wondered at that he should declare with emphasis that "my son [Benjamin] shall not go down with you; for his brother is dead, and he is left alone: if mischief befall him by the way in the which ye go, then shall ye bring down my gray hairs with sorrow to the grave."

They Must Not Take Benjamin

We can readily understand why the patriarch should speak in this way, and most certainly we sympathize with him. He did not know the real state of the case. He was thinking only of his sons. He was not thinking of God. In his whole statement there is no mention of God. He speaks to his sons as if they had done it all. "Me have ye bereaved of my children." "Then shall ye bring down my gray hairs with sorrow to the grave." He makes no reference to Him who one memorable night at

145

Bethel promised him, "I am with thee, and will keep thee in all places whither thou goest." For the moment Jacob had forgotten the mercies of God, forgotten the way the Lord had led him to Laban's house and given him prosperity during the years in Padan-aram, forgotten how the Lord had cared for him after the departure from Laban, forgotten the way God had brought about a reconciliation between himself and Esau, forgotten how He had blessed him at Penuel after the night-long wrestling, forgotten the divine protection when the violence of some of his sons might have made him a victim of the Shechemites.

Jacob Should Have Remembered

Jacob should have remembered that as God had seen him through all his former trials, so also He would be with him in the present one. If he had kept that in mind he would not have spoken as he did. Giving way to his fears as he did only made his trouble harder to bear, for he was bearing it without God.

However, his lapse was only temporary. After a while, as we shall see, he came back to his former trustfulness in God. When he came to bid farewell to his sons on their second journey to Egypt, this time accompanied by Benjamin, he was himself again, and prayed, "God Almighty give you mercy before the man, that he may send away your other brother, and Benjamin." Jacob had recovered himself. Before too long he came to see that instead of all these things being against him, they were in fact working together for his good. His tears and fears and forebodings were all wholly unnecessary, for they were called forth over the occurrence of evils that never came. They were in anticipation of events that never happened.

Reuben endeavored to reassure his father about Benjamin's safety if Jacob allowed him to be taken to Egypt. "Slay my two sons," he rashly said, "if I bring him not to thee: deliver him into my hand, and I will bring him to thee again." This impulsive speech did nothing to quiet Jacob's fears. He flatly refused to consent to Benjamin's being taken to Egypt.

But the days passed, and the supply of food brought from Egypt diminished, while the famine continued and became worse. When the grain they had was about exhausted, the sons of Jacob became convinced that they would have to go again to Egypt to replenish their supplies of grain. They were also convinced that such a journey would be futile unless they were allowed to take Benjamin with them. And they despaired of getting their father's consent to this. The situation seemed impossible. All they could do was to wait for their father to send them again to Egypt.

Jacob Yields Regarding Benjamin

The shadow of coming want and famine settled down upon them all. They went about with drawn and anxious faces, awaiting the decision of an old man who seemed inflexible. The time came when the old man saw suffering in their faces, and the fear of greater suffering in store. Finally the adamant will softened. He called his sons and pleaded, "Go again, buy us a little food."

Judah spoke for his brethren. He said to his father, "The man did solemnly protest unto us, saying, Ye shall not see my face, except your brother be with you. If thou wilt send our brother with us, we will go down and buy thee food: but if thou wilt not send him, we will not go down: for the man said unto us, Ye shall not see my face, except your brother be with you."

Thus the issue was joined. He would not let Benjamin go. They would not go without Benjamin. Jacob looked at them. They looked at him. And as they looked they became aware that his resolution was wavering. Judah took immediate advantage of it. He said, "Send the lad with me, and we will arise and go; that we may live, and not die, both we, and thou, and also our little ones. I will be surety for him; of my hand shalt thou require him: if I bring him not unto thee, and set him before thee, then let me bear the blame for ever: for except we had lingered, surely now we had returned this second time."

Jacob was the one who yielded. It was not easy for him to do so; but he knew they were right. Their provisions must be replenished or disaster faced them all. The situation demanded immediate remedy. They had already lost much time, as Judah pointed out. Having yielded, Jacob took charge of the planning for the trip, and for the diplomacy to be used to mollify the governor. Replying to Judah, Jacob said:

"If it must be so now, do this; take of the best fruits in the land in your vessels, and carry down the man a present, a little balm, and a little honey, spices, and myrrh, nuts, and almonds: and take double

147

money in your hand; and the money that was brought again in the mouth of your sacks, carry it again in your hand; peradventure it was an oversight."

Then he came to the main issue, and his voice grew solemn as he forced himself to say the words, "Take also your brother, and arise, go again unto the man." And this time God was in his thoughts, and the precious promises God had made him. "And God Almighty give you mercy before the man, that he may send away your other brother, and Benjamin. If I be bereaved of my children, I am bereaved."

A Touching Scene

It was a touching scene, this council between the old patriarch and his sons, as they consulted together regarding the means to be employed to obtain their three main objectives—the release of Simeon, the return of Benjamin, and another and adequate supply of food. They did not know that the heavy cloud of anxiety that pressed down upon their spirits and made them desperately uneasy was wholly uncalled for. They did not know that the dread governor of Egypt did not require any mollifying by them, but was entirely well disposed. They did not know that God had gone before them and made all the arrangements necessary for them to obtain all the desires of their hearts, and much more. They could not dream of the wonders into which they would walk on this journey to Egypt. They were to find their way to plenty, to blessedness, to nationhood, and to a magnificent future as they reluctantly turned their faces toward Egypt. In His omniscience and His mercy God had shut up every other door but the one through which it was His will for them to go. They had no alternative but to go down to Egypt.

Canaan was not yet ready for the children of Israel to enter into and possess. Nor were the children of Israel yet grown to that importance in numbers and resources that they needed to obtain and hold possession of the land. Time and opportunity were required for growth. Even when these were obtained they had to be put through the fire of trial and testing to be fused into a nation. It was for purposes such as these that they had to go down to Egypt and dwell there. These great purposes of God were far above their heads. They could not see them. They could only see what was directly before their eyes. And what they thus saw they did not like. They dreaded this trip to Egypt.

FULL SACKS AND MONEY BACK

A New Leadership

Before they began their journey there seemed to have emerged among them a new leadership, a change with no little significance for the future. The difference between the contrasting personalities and qualities of leadership of Reuben and Judah comes out strongly in their methods of dealing with their father. Reuben, the first-born, and as such the natural leader, made an impetuous proposal to Jacob, one that was wholly preposterous. "Slay my two sons," he said, "if I bring him [Benjamin] not to thee." He did not mean what he said. Its very rashness showed that he was not to be trusted.

Judah, on the other hand, did not make his sons surety for Benjamin. "I will be surety for him," he said. "Of my hand shalt thou require him: if I bring him not unto thee, and set him before thee, then let me bear the blame for ever." Not his sons but himself he pledged. And Jacob was convinced of his sincerity and his determination at all hazards to fulfill his pledge. And Judah later most nobly vindicated his father's confidence. It was Judah to whom Jacob consented to trust the remaining son of Rachel.

The whole encampment waved them away as they began their journey to Egypt—ten men with trepidation and foreboding in their hearts, not knowing what awaited them. That man, the governor. Would he believe them now that Benjamin was with them? Would he release Simeon? Would they be traveling back to Canaan on this road in a few days, a reunited family, every one accounted for? They did not dream what that accounting would include. And so they trudged onward toward Egypt, their minds troubled.

CHAPTER 24

In Egypt Before Joseph

FEARFUL as the brothers were, they made good progress toward Egypt. They pressed forward vigorously, as if to get this distasteful duty over as quickly as possible. The record declares, "The men took that present, and they took double money in their hand, and Benjamin; and rose up, and went down to Egypt, and stood before Joseph."

The brothers were surprised that the meeting with the governor was not as they feared a difficult one. He received them readily and kindly. His brusqueness was not in evidence. As they came into his presence his keen eye swept from one to another to make sure Benjamin was come. "And when Joseph saw Benjamin with them, he said to the ruler of his house, Bring these men home, and slay, and make ready; for these men shall dine with me at noon."

They were to be banqueted! And at the palace of the governor! They had not looked for anything like that. They should have been elated. This looked like an auspicious opening of their negotiations for the release of Simeon. But it was not elation they felt. It was fear. This was not normal. It was not understandable. It was mysterious. What trap was being laid for them now?

"And the men were afraid, because they were brought into Joseph's house." It made them uneasy to be ceremoniously ushered into an impressive palace. They looked about them with apprehension. The great rooms, the statuary, the furniture, the drapery—it was all far removed from their lowly tents, indeed from anything to which they were accustomed. They felt out of place, awkward, uncomfortable. They were not dressed for a banquet in this palace. They were out of their element. And their fears grew. They had not, they felt sure, been brought to this place just to eat. They had been brought here to be punished. Once again their consciences were awakened and plagued them about Joseph. As Joseph's major-domo left them alone they said:

"Because of the money that was returned in our sacks at the first time are we brought in; that he may seek occasion against us, and fall upon us, and take us for bondmen, and our asses."

What cowards does conscience make of us all! These men had guilt on their minds, their own guilt. That made it impossible for them to see anything in a clear light. Everything was distorted, twisted, frightening. They hastily concluded that they had better bring up this thing of the money in their sacks before Joseph made it the basis of any charge of dishonesty. They nervously awaited the return of his steward. When he came they said to him:

"O sir, we came indeed down at the first time to buy food: and it came to pass, when we came to the inn, that we opened our sacks, and, behold, every man's money was in the mouth of his sack, our money in full weight: and we have brought it again in our hand. And," they hurried on, "other money have we brought down in our hands to buy food: we cannot tell who put our money in our sacks." There! They had at least forestalled any charge of dishonesty by putting this thing straight. They felt it to be a smart move to make, to bring it up themselves.

"I Had Your Money"

And they were surprised beyond words at the response of the steward. He said, and I think he must have smiled as he said it, "Peace be unto you, fear not: your God, and the God of your father, hath given you treasure in your sacks: I had your money."

It took their breath. This steward, the governor's trusted servant, knew all about their money. He knew it had been put back in their sacks. He had had it. They did not know who did it. He knew, he told them. God did it. Their God, and their father's God. Well!

This was to be a banquet of surprises. The steward hurried away again, and when he returned he brought Simeon from the prison to join them. You can imagine the happy greetings, the exclamations, the clamor, the moving about, the inquiries about families, and about this banquet.

It was interrupted long before they could bring themselves up to date. The steward came to prepare them for the governor's arrival and for the banquet. They hurriedly got ready the present for the governor, which they had brought at Jacob's suggestion.

"And when Joseph came home, they brought him the present which was in their hand . . . and bowed themselves to him to the earth." That is, again they "made obeisance" to their brother as his long-ago dreams had foretold. Joseph could but think of those dreams as his brothers prostrated themselves before him. This was the moment they had dreaded, facing the governor once more. He had been harsh with them on the former occasion. Would he be again?

Joseph's Courtesy

They were pleasantly surprised at his agreeable manner. Most courteously he inquired regarding their health and well-being, and seemed genuinely interested. "He asked them of their welfare." They told him they were well and had had a safe journey. Then he expressed an interest in what they had found at home. "Is your father well, the old man of whom ye spake? Is he yet alive?" He hung upon the answer to that.

"And they answered, Thy servant our father is in good health, he is yet alive." And again "they bowed down their heads, and made obeisance." It was at this point that his glance again fell on Benjamin, the son of his own mother, and he said, "Is this your younger brother, of whom ye spake unto me?" When assured that it was even so, his overwhelming emotion allowed him to say only, "God be gracious unto thee, my son." Then he hurried out, for he knew he could stand no more for the moment. His very soul yearned over this younger brother of his. And he was not yet ready to make himself known to his brothers. There was too much more that he had to know about them. But one more moment in Benjamin's presence and he would have broken down and given everything away. And that must not happen yet.

So he made haste and got out of their sight. "He sought where to weep." There must be an outlet for the emotion that overmastered him. "And he entered into his chamber, and wept there." There are moments when tears are the only relief for overcharged emotions. This was one of the times. His brothers were left alone while he had a good spell of weeping. It had been twenty-two years or more since he had seen this childhood companion and playmate, now a grown man. Oh, how he loved this dear brother.

IN EGYPT BEFORE JOSEPH

Three Separate Tables

And then, his emotion at last under control, "he washed his face, and went out, and refrained himself [retained his self-control], and said, Set on bread." As there were caste laws in Egypt that did not permit Egyptians to eat with the people of other nations, with aliens, three separate tables were set. The Hebrews had a table by themselves. The Egyptians of Joseph's household were seated by themselves at another table. The governor, because of his superior rank, ate by himself, distributing the portions of all the foods as they were brought first to his own table.

When the eleven brothers were seated, and before the food was served, as they looked around the table at one another they were suddenly struck with amazement at discerning that they were seated and placed in the exact order of their age, "the firstborn according to his birthright, and the youngest according to his youth." Their astonished looks flew around the table and their brows knit with bewilderment. Who was well enough acquainted with them to do this?

But their attention was quickly drawn to another unusual thing. They did not know it, but from the moment of being seated at the table they were subjected to that ordeal of observation and testing that the governor designed to bring from them the information he was determined to obtain as to what sort of men they had become.

In the old days they had been madly jealous of him because his father had shown a partiality for him. He was sure his father had also shown, during the intervening years, a partiality for Benjamin. Had these men the same jealousy of Benjamin? He would test them on that point. He wanted to know whether, after selling him into slavery, there had been any change in his brothers, whether they had abandoned their evil ways. If it developed that they were just as jealous of Benjamin because partiality was shown him as they had been of Joseph, then he might determine to keep his younger brother by his side in Egypt rather than to let him return home. If it turned out that the old jealousy was gone and the old nature altered, then it might be possible to open the way for all his brothers, along with his old father, to join him in Egypt. He must first know whether they were the sort of men he wanted near him or whether they were the same kind of men he had known in the old days.

Their Jealousy Gone

He adopted a good way to find out. He began by sending over to Benjamin a portion from the food to be served that was five times larger than was sent to any of the others. That would do it. By this procedure he was showing a marked preference, nearly as much as his father had disclosed for him when he was given that princely garment of many colors. If these men were envious of Benjamin, this would bring it to the surface.

The brothers were still under the erroneous idea that Joseph was an Egyptian and could not understand them, so they did not hesitate to talk freely at the table, and in Joseph's hearing. Thus Joseph was presented with an excellent opportunity to discover their real feelings. He listened carefully, but no envious or spiteful remarks were heard. Indeed, the brothers seemed to be pleased that Benjamin was thus honored. These men were indeed changed. Joseph was deeply pleased. The banquet proceeded and became marked by the utmost harmony and gladness. The stiff formality with which it began melted away, giving place to friendly cordiality, the record saying, "They drank, and were merry with him."

But Joseph was not yet ready to disclose his identity to them. There was more he wanted to know about them before doing that. And he devised ways and means by which he could learn the answers to the questions he had in mind. He bade them farewell against their departure the next day and allowed them to go to their lodging places. They had many preparations to make before getting away in the morning.

A Group of Joyful Men

It was a group of joyful men that set out early the next morning on their journey home. The tension under which they had been for days was relaxed, and they were exuberant in their gladness that Simeon and Benjamin were with them. They would reach home a united group, and they hoped they were finished with Egypt for all time. Their beasts were laden with grain that would supply their needs for a long time to come. They had every reason for contentment with their situation. And added to everything else, they were homeward bound.

They did not know that the governor's steward, under the orders of his master, and under the appearance of being helpful in assisting in their departure preparations, had placed each man's money, the double money, again in his bag of grain, and in addition in Benjamin's bag had placed a silver drinking cup of special design. This cup was considered to possess the quality of detecting poison when any liquid containing poison was poured into it. Cups of this quality were much valued as safeguards against any attempt to murder their owners.

With light hearts Jacob's sons went on their way. They had scarcely cleared the outskirts of the city, however, when they became aware of the sounds of hasty pursuit. Joseph's steward, with all the appearance of suspicion, distrust, and scorn, caught up with them, stopped them, and scathingly inquired, "Wherefore have ye rewarded evil for good?" He proceeded to explain that his master's silver, and most valuable, drinking cup had disappeared with their departure and could be nowhere else but in their hands. He added, "Is not this it in which my lord drinketh, and whereby indeed he divineth? ye have done evil in so doing."

The Accusation Rejected

The sons of Jacob rejected this accusation with indignation. The steward was assuming too much when he charged them with such wickedness. They were no thieves. They had not purloined the governor's cup. They would not think of thus rewarding his kindness. And as evidence of their honesty they said, "God forbid that thy servants should do according to this thing: behold, the money, which we found in our sacks' mouths, we brought again unto thee out of the land of Canaan: how then should we steal out of thy lord's house silver or gold?" Such an accusation was outrageously false. They had demonstrated their honesty by bringing back the restored money.

Fine words, replied the steward, but somewhere in their luggage that cup was hidden. Were they willing to submit to a search? That would carry more weight than protestations of innocence.

Certainly, they angrily replied. He could search their goods as exhaustively as he desired. They were sure he would find nothing. Go ahead. And more, they were so certain of their innocence that "with whomsoever of thy servants it be found, both let him die, and we also will be my lord's bondmen."

A rash speech, indeed; a very rash speech. None of them knew what was in his own sack. And none knew what was in Benjamin's sack. But they were confident of one another's innocence of this wicked thing. Go ahead, search, they said; you are not going to find anything.

Very good, said the steward, that is fair enough. So "let it be according unto your words." However, I also want to be fair. Only "he with whom it is found shall be my servant; and ye shall be blameless."

Everybody being thus agreed, the search began without further delay. "They speedily took down every man his sack to the ground." And the steward, fully knowing what he would find, for he had placed it there himself, but wanting to stretch out the farce to its limits, began with Reuben's sack, intending to proceed from the oldest to the youngest, knowing that there the cup would make its appearance.

The Cup Found

You can imagine the shock of dismay that came to the outraged on-lookers when Reuben's sack disclosed the packet of double money, which they did not know was there. That was bad enough. But at any rate the silver cup did not show up. Slowly the steward went from bag to bag. In each one was the packet of money. And in Benjamin's sack, not only the money—but the silver cup!

The men looked at it, stunned, bewildered, speechless. Their whole world seemed to be tumbling about their ears. A few minutes before, they were going gladly back to their homes, to their father, to their children, with grain enough for all. Benjamin was with them. Simeon was singing for joy to be in the free air once more. They were pleasantly anticipating their father's happiness when he learned of Benjamin's safety, of Simeon's freedom, of the royal entertainment by the lord of Egypt, of how generously they had been treated. They felt as though in bringing Benjamin back they were almost compensating Jacob for having bereaved him of Joseph. Oh, they were happy.

And now, this! And of all things, Benjamin! They could not know he was innocent. Indeed, was this not proof that he was guilty? This, then, is that brother of theirs whom his father would not let out of his sight! This is the precious pet whose life was considered of more value than all the rest of them together! This is how this pampered favorite repays the anxiety of the family and their love. This is how, too, he repays the partiality and extraordinary favor of the governor! By this one rash, dishonest, childish act of thievery, this petted youth, at least to all appearance, brought upon the house and family of Jacob disgrace beyond remedy, perhaps complete extinction.

If these men had been the same men they were twenty-two years before, very likely their keen knives would have made short work of Benjamin. If they would not have gone so far as to kill him, they would have speedily turned him over to the steward, and to slavery. But the change that had taken place in their characters was revealed in the course they took.

They Stand by Benjamin

They were not disposed to turn their brother over to the steward and bring back to their old father another tale of blood. There was a consciousness that had come to them that this disaster had come upon them as a retribution for their sin against the other son of Rachel. They wanted no more of that. They were all guilty. They would stand united in punishment. Benjamin might be guilty. They thought he was. No matter; they would not let him suffer alone. They would share his punishment. They would stand by this younger brother of theirs.

As a token of their wretchedness "they rent their clothes." There could be no mistaking their sorrow. They were bowed down with grief. But they were not going to abandon their younger brother, no matter what he had done. No doubt Benjamin protested his innocence. But they did not listen. They seemed scarcely to consider whether he was innocent or guilty. In any case, he was their brother. His trouble was their trouble. It was no longer with them as it had been formerly. They were a family now, a united family, not merely individual units. They had learned their lesson and were humbled, God-smitten men. Once they had been quite indifferent to the sufferings of their father's favorite, and were wholly content to sell him into slavery. Not any more. They were sorry for Benjamin. Their hearts went out to him in brotherly feeling. Their mutual regard for their father had fused them into a family, and they did not propose to abandon a member of the family. They would stand together.

So they "laded every man his ass, and returned to the city." Joseph may have thought he would gain *one* brother by his strategem. Now he found himself with *eleven* on his hands.

CHAPTER 25

Joseph Reveals Himself

I T WAS a group of depressed and dismayed men who came to stand before Egypt's powerful governor. In his hands was the power of life
and death. They had been stopped as they were leaving the country and
charged with purloining his silver cup. There on the open road, as day
was dawning, they had been halted by his steward, they had been searched,
and the cup had been found in the sack of their youngest brother.

They did not know how it had gotten there. The steward said it had
been stolen, and they would have to return and face that charge before
the governor. Benjamin, though he declared himself innocent, seemed to
be guilty. They could not be sure of his innocence, and were inclined to
believe him guilty. However, they would not desert him. They all went
back to the governor's palace.

It was early morning, and Joseph had not yet left the house. Once more
these men prostrate themselves before him. They had thought not to see
him again. But here they all are once more in his presence, making obeisance to him. They were in the deepest distress, chagrined to be in a position of apparent guilt. Joseph spoke to them. (Because of its additional
clarity, I am using the Berkeley Version of the Bible.) He said:

" 'How could you do such a thing? Did you not know that a man like
me would unquestionably discover?' "

To this Judah, speaking for the group, replied:

" 'We do not know what to say to my master, or how to word our cause
so as to clear ourselves. God has exposed your servants' guilt. See, we are
my master's slaves, we as well as he with whom the cup is found.' "

Joseph would have none of that. " 'Not at all,' " he exclaimed. " 'I will
do no such thing. The person with whom the cup was found shall be my
slave, but you, you go up peacefully to your father.' "

They were free to go, ten of them. There was nothing to detain them, no charge laid against them. They could carry their grain back to their father and their families, where it was greatly needed. But they must go without Benjamin. He must remain in Egypt, and in slavery.

Mark the test here that Joseph was applying. So far as they knew, Benjamin was guilty and deserved his fate. He had brought it on himself. They had no share in it. Would these ten brothers go back to their homes and leave Benjamin alone, in the grasp of Egyptian justice, to take the punishment he clearly deserved? That was what Joseph wanted to know. Twenty-two years earlier they would not have thought twice over such a decision. They had sold Joseph into slavery when they knew him innocent. Would they treat Benjamin, whom they thought guilty, any differently? Were they the same men or were they different men? Joseph waited to see.

Judah's Noble Speech

Now follows one of the finest scenes in all the range of literature. These men do not propose to go off and leave Benjamin alone. They have weighed the matter and they are going to stand by their brother. They have no interest in going home without him. If they go, he must go with them. If he is held, they will share his fate. Moreover, they cannot contemplate going to their father without his favorite. They know that would bring death to the old man. Twenty-two years before they would not have cared. They sold Joseph away from him. But no more of that sort of thing for them. They loved their father, and they loved Benjamin. They would stand together. The plea that Judah now makes has no match for nobility and for natural eloquence in the world's literature in any language, sacred or profane. The Berkeley Version has it:

"Judah then stepped up to him and said, 'With your permission, my master, your servant would tell you something intimate, and let not your anger blaze against your servants, for you are Pharaoh's counterpart. My master asked his servants, "Do you still have a father or a brother?" So we told my master, "We have an aged father and a young brother, a child of his old age; his brother is dead, so he alone remains of his mother, and his father loves him!" Then you told your servants, "Bring him down to me, so I may see him!" But we said to my master, "The lad cannot leave his father; should he leave him, his father would die." Upon which you

159

told your servants, "If your youngest brother does not come down with you, you shall not see my face again."

" 'On our return to your servant my father, we gave him my master's message, and when our father said, "Go back to buy us a little food," we answered, "We cannot go down. If our youngest brother is with us we will go down; for we cannot meet the man unless our youngest brother goes with us."

" 'Your servant our father said to us, "You know that my wife bore me two sons. One left me and I said, Yes, he is surely torn to pieces and I have not seen him since. If you take this one, too, and something happens to him, you will bring down my gray hairs to Sheol with sorrow!" Now then, since his life is bound up in the lad's life—when I come to my father and the lad is not with us, he will die, and your servants will be bringing the hoary head of your servant my father with sorrow to the grave. But your servant went guaranty for the lad to my father, saying, "If I fail to bring him back to you, then I will bear the blame before my father forever." I beg of you, therefore, to retain your servant in the lad's place, a slave to my master, and let the lad go up with his brothers; for how could I go up to my father and not have the lad with me! To witness the grief my father must suffer!' "

" 'I Am Joseph!' "

That did it! It is quite likely that if such a plea had been made before any ordinary Egyptian official it would have gained its end. Joseph was ready to end all his pretense, throw off his masquerade, disclose his identity, and take these dear brothers to his heart. They had proved themselves to be true men. He could trust them now. He was shaken with emotion. His very soul was moved to its depths. His brothers had repented of what they had done to him and what they had done to their father. Their conduct proved their penitence to be wholly sincere. He ordered everyone but his brothers out of the room, and when he was alone with his brethren the record is, "So loudly did he weep that the Egyptians and Pharaoh's household heard it." He cried out, " 'I am Joseph! Is my father still alive?' "

His brothers shrank back with a sense of acute dismay. They were stunned, amazed beyond words. They could find no words to answer him. They could only stare. He spoke to them again:

"'Please, come close to me.'" And as they edged nearer, he said, "'I am Joseph, your brother, whom you sold into Egypt.'"

Now it was coming, they felt sure. He had not overlooked what they had done. Their guilt was in his mind. And he had them in his power. They had terribly wronged him. What would their punishment be? But his next words straightened them out.

He Comforts Them

"'Be not disheartened or vexed with yourselves for selling me here, because God sent me ahead of you to save your life.'"

That was certainly an aspect of their conduct that had escaped their notice. Joseph's voice was actually gentle; he was pleading with them. He was not angry. God had been in all this, he said.

He continued:

"'For two years now the famine is in the land and there are five more years without plowing or harvest, and God sent me before you to assure for you continuance on the earth; to grant you survival through a great salvation. So then, you did not send me here, but God, and He has appointed me a father to Pharaoh, a master of his whole palace and ruler over all Egypt.'"

They were breathing easier. Could it be he had no thought of punishing them? That seemed incredible. Nothing like this had ever been known. They hung on his next words.

"'Hurry and go up to my father and tell him, "This is your son Joseph's message: God has put me in charge of all Egypt. Come down to me without delay. You will live in the land of Goshen where you will be near me, you, your children and your grandchildren, your flocks, your herds and everything you have. There I will support you, so that you, your family and all you possess may not suffer privation—for there are five more years of famine."'"

That was his message to be borne by them to his father. Now, seeing they were having extreme difficulty in believing the evidence of their senses, in believing this was really their own brother, Joseph, he said:

"'Take note! You see for yourselves and so does my brother Benjamin, that I am personally conversing with you; and tell my father about all my splendor in Egypt, and everything you have observed. Hurry and bring my father down here.'"

161

The Long-sundered Family Reunited

With that he went straight to Benjamin, threw his arms about him, and wept. Benjamin embraced him, and they wept together a long time before they could compose themselves. Then Joseph kissed them all and embraced them as he wept with them. The family was united again. Love ran from heart to heart. Their separation was over.

Joseph was fully satisfied. He had put his brothers to the test. They had met the test magnificently. Their sin had been abundantly confessed. He had been particularly desirous of knowing what their feelings were toward Benjamin, to compare them with what he knew their feelings had been toward himself so long ago. He had tried them in various ways. They had been aroused to intense jealousy and hatred in his own case when his father showed partiality for him. So he treated Benjamin better than the others. And they did not show resentment. It was Benjamin, so they thought, who had now brought all this trouble upon them. They did not abandon him to his fate, much as they thought he deserved it. They knew how to forgive. They knew how to love. They knew how to forbear. They had no malice toward their young brother. And they had supreme affection toward their old father. They were not going to have him hurt. They had terribly hurt him once. Not any more. All Joseph's purposes were carried out. All his conditions were fulfilled. He had learned what he set out to discover. He was satisfied.

With their tears flowing freely, and locked in each other's arms, they had a time of reconciliation. He kissed them all. All? Yes, all. Simeon, the cruel one, who was the instigator of the crime against Joseph? Yes, Simeon. And Reuben, the unstable one. And Benjamin, the blameless one. And Judah, who at the pit's mouth had gotten the brothers' minds away from their first thought of murder. All of them, forgiven and reconciled.

"After that his brethren talked with him." They had been speechless during most of this marvelous scene. Now they had their brother back. They had freely confessed their sin against him. They had sought his forgiveness. It had as freely been given. Their long remorse had ended. They could talk now. It was so good to know that he was alive, so good to have the long-broken family reunited, so good to find him lord of all Egypt. What a story they would have to tell their father!

162

JOSEPH REVEALS HIMSELF

Pharaoh Greatly Pleased

And so they talked and planned and arranged, and saw great visions of the future. And while they talked, the news of what had taken place had gotten out, and was spreading like fire in stubble. It had penetrated to the palace of Pharaoh and was brought to the king. He was mightily pleased. He had been moved for some time by a sense of profound gratitude to Joseph for his services to the nation. Here was his chance to show it. He sent word to say to the men from Canaan, "The good of the land of Egypt" is yours. He seconded Joseph's invitation to Jacob and to his brothers to move from Canaan to Egypt and bring their families and beasts and all their possessions with them.

And now the time came for the brothers to be off for home. They had great messages to deliver to their father, from Egypt's Pharaoh as well as from Egypt's premier, and their eagerness to do so was great. The caravan Joseph organized and supplied for them surpassed anything they could have dreamed. Wagons, carriages, servants, beasts, everything that was necessary for the transportation of three-score and ten persons, with their household goods, and all other possessions. They were supplied with abundant provision for the journey, going and returning. And on Benjamin, Joseph bestowed again more gifts than on the others.

And knowing these men well, he called after them a parting admonition, "See that ye fall not out by the way."

CHAPTER 26

"Joseph My Son Is Yet Alive"

HIGHLY elated men they were, these brothers of Joseph, as they started out from Egypt to return to Canaan and the encampment of their father. What a story they had to tell! What a message they were charged with! How joyous their father would be! Benjamin was with them. Simeon was with them. And Joseph was alive. It all seemed too good to be true.

They were leading an imposing and lengthy array of camels, asses, and wagons. The wagons were laden with the best that Egypt could provide. Pharaoh had joined with Joseph in arranging for this wagon train. He had given them changes of raiment, talents of silver, and sent along all the provisions they would need for the way. These men had found a fortune in Egypt. More than that, they had found their long-lost brother. Better than that, this long-lost brother had turned out to be their savior and the savior of their families. Best of all, he had been reconciled to them. There was no longer any breach between them. He had forgiven them the deadly wrong they had done him. The weight under which their consciences had groaned for these many years was lifted. They were jubilant men as they hurried toward home to tell all the wonderful story to their father.

Jacob Must Be Told

Ah, yes, their father! They had some things to make right there, too. They had done him a grave wrong. It was not only the story of Joseph in Egypt they were going to have to tell their father. There was more than that he had to know. There was how Joseph got to Egypt. There was the pit, and the sale into slavery, and his pleadings, and the dipping of his coat in blood, and the deception, and the big lie. Jacob was going to have to be told all that, too. It could not be hid any longer. It had already been kept under cover too long. They would be glad when it was all laid out before Jacob. Then it would be done with. Joseph had forgiven them. They believed their father would also forgive.

And so they drew near the encampment of Jacob. They had been seen, and the news had been carried to the old man in his tent that his sons were returning from Egypt. Nothing was said about the long train of wagons and camels and asses. Jacob's heart beat faster. Benjamin? Simeon? Was all well? He awaited their arrival with growing impatience.

At last they crowded into his presence, bursting out with amazing news: "Joseph is yet alive, and he is governor over all the land of Egypt!" It was too much for Jacob. It overwhelmed him. He did not believe them. "Jacob's heart fainted." Something strange had come over these sons of his to make them say such fantastic things. He would ignore it, and perhaps they would come to their senses.

Benjamin! Oh, yes, Benjamin was with them, and he stepped forward and greeted his father lovingly. But then he too began to babble about Joseph, what Joseph had said, what Joseph had sent, what Joseph had ordered. He put Benjamin aside. Were all his sons beside themselves?

Simeon? Yes, Simeon had been set free and was here. Simeon came forward and greeted his father. And, of all things, he too began to chatter about Joseph, how Joseph had treated him, about a banquet at Joseph's house, how Joseph had set him free, and how Joseph had bidden them all move down to Egypt. Jacob was getting irritated. What had gotten into these men? Benjamin's return he could accept—and be thankful for. And Simeon's. But Joseph, who for twenty-two years he had mourned as dead! It disturbed him.

Joseph Is Still Alive!

And then, doubtless, sensing the depth of his bewilderment, one of his sons, said, "Father, come outside, and see." And they led him out. And he looked and saw that long line of wagons, equipment such as only royalty and the very wealthy could possess. There, too, was the long train of camels, and she asses, all loaded down with the good things of Egypt. He was shown the changes of raiment, the silver, the provisions. Again he was overwhelmed—and convinced. His spirit revived. He began to grasp the immensity of this amazing thing. And he exclaimed:

"Well, this is different! I can believe it now. Yes, this is just like Joseph. He would do a thing like this. Joseph, my son, is still alive! Very well, I will go and see him before I die."

They led him back into the tent, dazed by the greatness of this development, trying to reach out and take it all in. It was stupendous! Joseph alive! Joseph, lord of all Egypt! Joseph bidding him to move to Egypt! Joseph encouraging him to come and be taken care of, to have all his needs supplied, to live in the most fruitful part of Egypt!

"Tell me," he cried out, "what did he say, what did my son Joseph say?"

So they began the long story that he never tired of hearing. "Thus saith thy son, Joseph." Ah yes. From Joseph. There was nothing second-handed about this. It was straight from Joseph. "We have seen him," they said. "We have talked with him. He spoke to us. The word we bring you is from Joseph himself. Thus saith thy son Joseph."

What Joseph Said

What did Joseph say? "Tell him," Joseph had said, "tell my father that God hath exalted me and made me governor over all the land of Egypt. Tell him that hanging at my girdle are the keys to the storehouses of all Egypt. Tell him that the wealth of the greatest of earthly nations is at the disposal of the one whom he has long mourned for dead. Tell him that Joseph is alive."

"Oh, yes," they said, "Joseph had more for us to tell you. And this is something we would prefer not to tell. But it must be told some time, and perhaps it is as well to tell it now."

"What is that?"

"The governor, your son Joseph, said, 'You may tell my father how all this came to pass. Tell him I was sold as a slave. Do not hide from him that it was you yourselves who sold me for silver. Tell him about that coat of mine. Tell him I was cast into a dungeon. Tell him that I came out of prison, and I was exalted to the throne of the Pharaohs, sharing the throne with the mightiest of all monarchs. Tell him I wear upon my hand the signet ring of his supreme authority. Tell my father all this when you get home. That is what has come to pass with Joseph.

" 'Then tell my father how the storehouses were built and filled,

166

about the years of abundance and the years of famine. Tell him how all nations of the earth have to come to me if they would be fed, if they would be delivered from famine, just as you have come. Tell my father that, and tell him that the storehouses are so full that I had to leave off counting the amount of grain they hold, as it has become past numbering.

" 'And there is more that you are to tell my father, and this is it: Ye shall tell my father of all my glory in Egypt, and of all that ye have seen; and ye shall haste and bring down my father hither.

" 'Tell my father of all that ye have seen. You sat at my table. You came into my palace. You partook of my hospitality. You ate of my provisions. You have seen the glories of earth's greatest empire. When you get home tell my father that I am governor over it all. And tell him it is all for him. I want him to share it all with me. Tell him, too, that God sent me before you to preserve you a posterity in the earth. Tell him that, and urge him to come with all speed, to see what here awaits him.

" 'And tell my father more. Tell him that only two years of the seven famine years have passed. There are to be five more. And in these five years there will be neither plowing nor harvest. The famine is going to grow so desperate that the only places on earth where grain can be had will be in my storehouses. Tell my father that he must come. The only way to save our people is for him to come. Tell him there is no other way out. He cannot do without me. No one else can help him.

Come Down to Egypt

" 'Moreover, when you get back home you will look at all you own and find a lot of things you will not want to leave behind. Some of you will say that it is going to cost you a lot to go down to Egypt. You are wrong. Pharaoh sends this message to my father and you: "Regard not your stuff; for the good of all the land of Egypt is yours." So say to my father: "Make haste. Come down to me. Tarry not. Come—come—come! " ' "

"Joseph said that?"

"Yes, father, Joseph said that. He wants you with him in Egypt. He wants you to go down to him with all you have, and all of us with you, with all our families and beasts and belongings. And he will put us in the Goshen Delta, a well-watered, most fertile part of Egypt. Moreover,

167

the Pharaoh joined your son Joseph in this invitation. He it was who provided these wagons, these changes of raiment, these provisions, in order that the moving may be made easy."

We can scarcely wonder that when Jacob heard this wonderful narrative he could not grasp it all. It certainly was an amazing story. But was it not also only a lovely dream? These men, his sons, had been deceiving him during more than a score of years. Might they not now be deceiving him? It might be all right to go down to Egypt and see Joseph, now that he had learned he was alive. But to move there! To stay there! That was something different. God had told him that He would give him this land of Canaan for an everlasting possession. What business had he going to Egypt?

It could be that his sons might want to go to Egypt for purposes they were concealing from him. He thought again of their former deceptions. It might be that they had invented this Joseph story to break down the resistance they knew he would feel to any suggestion of a migration into Egypt. They were capable of it, as he well knew. He had better look into this thing a little further. He had consented to go to Egypt to see Joseph. But just suppose there were no Joseph in Egypt! What was it that had made him so ready to agree to go and see Joseph? Oh, yes. The wagons. He would take another look at those wagons.

"See here, my sons. It seems strange to me that my son Joseph would have sent me such a message as you bring from him. You must have told him how frail I am, and he knows how old I am. If this governor you talk about is really my son Joseph, he should understand what an impossibility it is for a man of my age with my many infirmities to make such a long journey. It does not sound like Joseph. Are you sure this man is my son? It cannot be Joseph. If it were he would be touched with a feeling of my infirmities. Let me look at those wagons again."

This Is Like Joseph

So they led him out once more. "What are these?" he asked. "Camels." They were still loaded. They bore the great quantity of grain Joseph had sent. "And these?" "This, Father, is a train of asses laden with the good things of Egypt that Joseph has sent you." "And this long line of wagons—these luxurious wagons?" "These wagons, Father, are those that Joseph sent to carry you to Egypt. He did think of your infirmities.

He knew the journey would be a hard one for you. To lighten it so there would be no walking for you, and no riding upon camel or ass, he sent these wagons. You will be carried without effort, together with the women and children. Joseph thought of everything."

The old man was convinced. "I see! I see! This is different. Indeed, it is just like Joseph. Bless my son, my well-beloved. He must be alive. I will indeed go and see him before I die. But move to Egypt! I am not sure about that. God has told me Canaan is to be my country. I must think more of this."

Jacob was troubled. Joseph had spoken. Pharaoh had spoken. His sons had spoken. And they all united in telling him to go down to Egypt. But God had not spoken—except on that former occasion when Jacob had been told that Canaan was to be his future home.

It was not long, however, before all this was changed. In "visions of the night" God came to him and said, "Jacob, Jacob."

"Here am I," Jacob answered.

"I am God, the God of thy father: fear not to go down into Egypt; for I will there make of thee a great nation: I will go down with thee into Egypt; and I will surely bring thee up again: and Joseph shall put his hand upon thine eyes."

That gracious word settled it for Jacob. Truly Joseph was alive. This was no trick, no deception. He was disturbed no more. His mind, his heart, were at rest. God was in this. So everything was all right. And he would embrace Joseph once more. God was good to him in his old age. Benjamin had returned. Simeon was home. His sons were changed men. They had asked his forgiveness, and he had given it. The long-sundered family was to be united once again, not one missing. And he was going to Joseph and would see his glory. Oh, God was good!

Jacob Comes to Egypt

And the record is, "The sons of Israel conveyed their father Jacob, their little ones and their wives in the wagons Pharaoh had sent to convey him. They took their cattle and their movable belongings, which they had accumulated in Canaan, and arrived in Egypt, Jacob and all his descendants with him—his sons, his grandsons, his daughters, his grand-daughters—all his descendants he brought with him to Egypt."

How marvelously through the years God had worked to bring it all

169

about! Everything had worked together—bad men with bad motives, jealousy, hatred, malice, slavery, deception, atrocious lies, imprisonment, neglect, cruel forgetfulness, dreams, royalty, courtiers, national prosperity, national calamity—all things had worked together at the right time to fulfill God's purposes. They always have; they always do; they always will.

God wanted His people down in Egypt for a time. There were great obstacles in the way. But all things were in God's hands; all things were under His control. He knew how to make them all combine to accomplish His will. That caravan, that imposing train of wagons on its way to Egypt, is evidence of the profound truth that "all things work together for good to them that love God."

CHAPTER 27

Jacob Goes to Egypt

J ACOB and his eleven sons, with the members of their families, together with their flocks and herds as well as numerous attendants,
were before long ready to set out on the exciting migration to Egypt. It
was with gladness of heart that they had made all the preparations for
this momentous journey. They recognized its necessity if they were to
be delivered from the perils of the continuing and worsening famine.
Their brother, with whom a thorough reconciliation had been brought
about, was in charge of all Egypt and in a position to give them shelter
and sustenance. They were eager to be off on the great adventure that
was to provide them a new home.

They made short work of their preparations to get started. Their
cherished household possessions they carefully packed and stored in the
long line of wagons that Pharaoh had sent for that purpose. In these
wagons, too, they arranged places for Jacob and the women and children.
Transportation by wagon was something new. It is quite unlikely that
at that time wagons were used or even known in Palestine. Some of the
monuments, it is true, depict a common kind of wagon having two
wheels, which at the time was used in Egypt but had not found its way
elsewhere. But these wagons from Egypt, sent for the comfort of Jacob,
were something new, of a superior make, covered to shade their occupants from the sun and the elements. They gave the caravan an impressive appearance as it started out from Hebron.

Beer-sheba and Memories

They came quickly to Beer-sheba. This was on the very edge of
Canaan, just where it blends into the desert. Beer-sheba was a place
that awakened many memories in Jacob's mind. It not only had associa-

171

tions for himself but memories of his father and grandfather as well. It was at Beer-sheba that Abraham had planted a grove and called upon the name of the Lord, the Eternal. There too Isaac had had his encampment for many years.

It was but natural, therefore, that he should stop the caravan at Beer-sheba for purposes of worship. He offered sacrifices; he made supplication; he asked special enlightenment about this journey into Egypt. And it was here that he received assurance that God would go with him into Egypt and that there God would make him into a great nation, and would surely bring him up again. It was with this gracious reassurance that they all resumed their journey.

It has been pointed out that it was not without considerable misgivings that Jacob had consented to abandon Canaan for Egypt. The land of Canaan had a peculiar interest for him. It was the land of promise. God had made a covenant regarding this land with him. He had, it is true, spent twenty-one years of his life outside its borders. But it was with renewed faith that he had come back to it, faith that it was yet to be his own. Notwithstanding the great pull at his heart now to go into Egypt and clasp his long-lost Joseph to his breast, it was nevertheless a trial for him to leave Canaan. Canaan had in it the Cave of Machpelah, where the bodies of Isaac and Abraham slept. It was not easy to leave them behind. In addition to everything else, Egypt had always been an unpropitious place for the Israelites. Both Isaac and Abraham had sojourned there briefly, with unfortunate results.

The New Home

Consequently he was greatly cheered to receive reassurance from God that it was all right for him to go into Egypt. From Beer-sheba he went forward with an easier heart. He began with increasing eagerness to anticipate the great moment when he would be reunited with his beloved Joseph.

Jacob and his sons had been instructed to go directly to Goshen. This was an area in the northeast of Lower Egypt. One branch of the Nile bounded it on the west, the desert shut it in on the east, the Mediterranean was on the north, and it is considered probable that it extended south as far as to the head of the Red Sea. Pharaoh's dominion extended over it, and it was therefore in Egypt, but scarcely of it, for it was little more than on the confines of the country. It was a land of pasturage, most suitable for the feeding of herds and flocks. It was the nearest part of Egypt to Canaan. It was not far from Joseph's residence. It was very likely for these reasons that Joseph looked upon it as the most advantageous section of Egypt for Jacob and his sons.

At Beer-sheba God had said to Jacob, "Fear not to go down into Egypt; for I will *there* make of thee a great nation." This was of great significance. To Abraham had been given a promise of a posterity that should be so numerous as to be beyond numbering. There had been no evidence that such a promise was being fulfilled. Abraham's posterity numbered but three-score persons. Its enlargement was scarcely perceptible. Nor could they experience any great enlargement in Canaan without peril and hardship and war. There was no room for them to become numerous in Canaan. This land was in the possession of powerful, warlike tribes who would fight before being pushed aside. They were not to be dispossessed until "the fourth generation." Their time had not yet come. Israel could not multiply into greatness in Canaan.

But Egypt was different. It offered conditions such as would be necessary for the fulfillment of God's purpose. Goshen was well-watered, excessively fertile, and afforded every opportunity for their speedy increase. And they could be shut off there by themselves. Every shepherd was "an abomination to the Egyptians." For that reason there would be no social intermingling, no intermarrying. They could remain distinct, separate, alone, apart from Egypt and its idolatry. It was to gain for them this opportunity that Joseph had been sent before them into Egypt and placed in such a position of power and influence that he could make this land available to them.

Father and Son Meet

When the caravan drew near the borders of Egypt, Jacob sent Judah to let Joseph know of their approach, and to request instructions in greater detail as to how they should proceed. Joseph did not send instructions. When he learned of his father's nearness, his heart leaped, and he went out himself to meet him. In his chariot of state and accompanied by a princely retinue, he raced forward to meet his father, his heart filled with eagerness, love, and tenderness.

These two had not seen each other for twenty-two years; they had parted when Joseph left his father's encampment with a cheery wave of farewell to go and look for his brothers. Joseph was then a lad of seventeen. Now he was thirty-nine, and the executive head of all Egypt. This was one of the great moments of his life. He was going to take his old father once more into his embrace, and cherish him the rest of his life.

He completely forgot the splendor that surrounded him, and the exalted position he held. He was no longer governor of Egypt. He was the son of Jacob. He had but one thought, one great longing. His heart thrilled with intense yearning to see his father. And when he caught sight of the long line of wagons in the distance, his eagerness knew no bounds. He ordered his charioteer to greater speed; his eagerness was now no longer under control. Joseph dashed up to the wagon in the lead, which had stopped and from which a feeble old man was climbing down, leaped from his chariot, and hurried to his father to bid him welcome and express his greetings in words that he had been putting together for some time.

The words were not spoken. As these two looked into each other's eyes, their emotions overcame them. Words were too feeble to express the feelings that swept like overwhelming waves over their souls. They fell into each other's arms and remained there for a long time, while the Egyptian courtiers and the sons of Jacob looked on the scene with streaming eyes. The record says, "And he [Joseph] fell on his neck, and wept on his neck a good while." And, oh, the thoughts that must have raced through their minds as they clung together in loving embrace. And finally Jacob gently disengaged himself, pushed his beloved Joseph far enough away to look at him from head to feet, and feasted his eyes on this boy he loved so well. Only then did he speak. What he said was "Now let me die, since I have seen thy face, because thou art yet alive." Did he, perchance, recall his doleful lament of not long before, "All these things are against me"?

Presenting His Father and Brothers

Joseph then proudly presented his father to the members of the nobility who composed his retinue. He also made them acquainted with his brothers. After all the greetings and salutations were completed, Joseph called his brothers together for some special information and guidance. He planned, he said, to take some of them, not all, five perhaps would be sufficient, to present to Pharaoh. He had a clear idea of the questions the king would ask them, and he wanted to counsel with them regarding their answers. He would inquire as to their occupation. It was important that they should make it plain that they were shepherds. That would be the exact truth, and it would serve also to obtain for them a settlement away from the other inhabitants of Egypt, in a district where they could be by themselves, not entangled by alliances and associations with the Egyptians; and most important of all, not brought into contact with the corrupting influences of the idolatries of the land. Egyptians were prejudiced against shepherds, and their occupation would serve as a wall of separation to isolate them from both the contempt with which Joseph knew the Egyptians would treat them and the degrading contamination of the prevailing idolatry. Moreover, it would contribute much toward obtaining for them the very desirable territory of the Goshen Delta.

When he took them in to present them to Pharaoh they followed his instructions carefully. Indeed, they went so far as to request that because of their occupation, and for the sake of their flocks, they might have the king's permission to establish themselves in Goshen. Their request was granted at once, and the king commanded Joseph, if he approved and if he knew any of his brothers who were qualified for the office, to give them charge of the royal herds.

Jacob and Pharaoh

After that audience had thus issued so auspiciously, Joseph with the deepest pride and affection led his venerable father into the royal presence and presented him to Pharaoh. It was a memorable interview. I do not know of another comparable with it. On the throne the most powerful monarch of his time; by his side the ablest statesman of his age, who even then was skillfully guiding Egypt through the fearful calamity of famine; and before them the oldest saint on the earth, heir to the promises made by Jehovah to Abraham and Isaac. Not before that time, and not since, has there been the meeting of such a trio.

Jacob was respectful. But that respect was manifested in ways not customarily seen in presentations at court. He begins the interview with a benediction. He ends it with another. He did not hide his religion. He used it to glorify what would otherwise have been a commonplace interview. He manifested his faith in such a way as to make it contribute to the royal welfare by asking for the king the favor of the true God. He is not abashed before royalty. He himself had seen the King of kings, face to face. He does not presume because of that to admonish the king, but shows his religion by blessing him.

The king availed himself of the privilege of asking the most natural question under the circumstances. "How old art thou?" And Jacob made answer, "The days of the years of my pilgrimage are an hundred and thirty years: few and evil have the days of the years of my life been, and have not attained unto the days of the years of the life of my fathers in the days of their pilgrimage." The writer of the Epistle to the Hebrews must have had this reply in mind when he wrote of the patriarchs confessing "that they were strangers and pilgrims."

The Prince of God and the King of Egypt

Jacob had certainly been a pilgrim. He had spent twenty-one years a stranger in Padan-aram. When he returned to Canaan he had still wandered about from place to place. "Few and evil," he said, had been his years. Few in the sense that his fathers had attained an age greater than his. Terah had lived to be 205; Abraham 175; Isaac 180; Jacob was only 130 when he stood before Pharaoh. "So the whole age of Jacob was an hundred forty and seven years."

His years had been evil in the sense of being hard and filled with trial. He had been separated from his home and had gone forth into exile to spend his best years as a stranger in a strange land. His service to Laban was filled with hardship, consumed in the day by heat and in the night by frost. It was with great difficulty that he got away from Laban. Then he found it necessary to meet his incensed and impetuous brother. It was in the agony of that dreadful crisis that he encountered the Angel Wrestler. The sinew of his thigh was touched by the Divine Visitor, and all his life since then he had suffered a limp. Extreme danger came to him at Shechem, danger that whitened his hair, furrowed his cheeks, scarred his heart. He lost his beloved Rachel at Ephrath. His later sorrows we have already witnessed in the loss of his beloved Joseph and the dissensions of his wild sons.

Few and evil. Yet when this patriarch comes to stand before the greatest monarch on earth, that monarch bends eagerly to receive his

176

blessing. "Jacob blessed Pharaoh." "Without . . . contradiction the less is blessed of the better." Quite clearly, therefore, Jacob was a greater man than the greatest monarch of his time. God Himself had said to him, "Thy name shall be called no more Jacob, but Israel [a prince of God]: for as a prince hast thou power with God and with men, and hast prevailed."

And thus Jacob came to Egypt, and with his sons settled in Goshen. There they grew into the nation that God had planned.

CHAPTER 28

Joseph and His Father

WHEN Jacob had first gathered Joseph in his arms on his arrival in Egypt he felt that life was as full as he could reasonably expect, and he had exclaimed, "Now let me die." There was nothing in life for which he cared to live beyond reunion with his beloved Joseph. However, seventeen years more of life came to him. They were the most contented, most peaceful years of his life, and filled with the satisfaction of constant fellowship with his favorite son, the mighty prime minister of Egypt.

The record we have been following tells us very little of Joseph's experience and affairs during these years. It is evident, however, that he remained in his exalted station in Egypt, even though the immediate need for his special services as food administrator passed away with the famine years. He was still a great figure in the land, the savior of Egypt, and the people and the nobles held him in high esteem. His prosperity was shared by his kinsmen, who continued to dwell in the Goshen Delta.

There are but two incidents belonging to these seventeen years that are of interest to our story. These are connected with the closing years of Jacob's life, which were made joyous by the fellowship of, and free of care by the kindness of, his beloved Joseph. The first of these incidents was an interview between father and son alone. Jacob had come to feel that his days on earth were soon to close. The infirmities of age increasingly troubled him. His thoughts turned more and more from the things of this world and fixed upon the world to come. He thought much of his departure. He must soon "be gathered to his fathers." He believed his descendants some day would return to Canaan, the covenant Land of Promise. He could discern no evidence that such a return would come at any early date. Israel had not grown to such proportions that it could reasonably expect to dispossess the Canaanites. Quite clearly Joseph had yet work to do in Egypt. His other sons were too prosperous and too comfortable in Egypt to have any incentive to move. It became clear to Jacob that his death would take place in Egypt.

Burial in the Promised Land

He gave much thought to the effect his death was likely to have on the faith and the character of his descendants. If he were buried in Egypt without giving any instructions about God's promise and God's covenant, in which Jehovah had pledged Himself to give Canaan to his posterity, would that not appear like relinquishing his claim to the Land of Promise entirely? Might it not reconcile his descendants to remaining in Egypt permanently?

Such a possibility brought Jacob much mental distress. He had a duty to perform, a testimony to give. It was then that he summoned Joseph, whom he knew he could trust implicitly. Jacob required of Joseph a promise, administered by an oath, that his remains should not be buried in Egypt. Instead, they were to be carried up out of Egypt to Canaan, and laid in the Cave of Machpelah, where he could sleep alongside Abraham and Sarah, Isaac and Rebekah, and his own Leah.

It must not be thought that this request grew merely out of the natural desire that any man may have for his body to rest beside those of his own people. It was something far more than that which moved Jacob. The land of Canaan, by God's covenant, was his. It was not yet his in reality. He had not yet obtained it. It was his by promise. He believed that promise. It seemed clear to him now that he would die before he obtained it. No doubt he would die in Egypt without entering into possession of the Promised Land.

Egypt Not Their Home

Even in such a death he greatly desired to leave a witness to his children, to his posterity, that he retained his confidence that his descendants would have ownership, possession, of Canaan. It was because of this that he had Joseph swear to take his remains and bury them in the sepulcher of his fathers. He would thus witness to the world of his implicit belief in the promises of God and the future of his posterity.

There was more he had in mind. He wanted his sons and all his

179

descendants to be constantly aware that Egypt was not their home, not their permanent place of residence. They must never look upon it as their future inheritance. They did not belong in Egypt. Canaan was their Land of Promise. He wanted to fix their minds, their hopes, on Canaan, to kindle in their souls a fervent love of their homeland, to keep alive their determination to return there when God's time came for them to do so, and when He should open the way. He would have nothing hold them in Egypt; he would emphasize everything that would incite them to go back to Canaan. He would be buried there himself to deepen their interest, to strengthen their enthusiasm. These are the reasons underlying his request to Joseph, "Bury me not . . . in Egypt: but I will lie with my fathers, . . . bury me in their burying place."

Joseph was quite ready to comply with his father's wishes. "I will do as thou hast said." Jacob's anxiety on this point was thus wholly removed. He knew Joseph would do as he promised.

The Final Interview

There was another interview between Joseph and Jacob which took place just before the latter's death. There were two others present, Joseph's sons, Ephraim and Manasseh. A message reached Joseph that his father was ill, and with his two sons he hurried to his father's bedside. They told Jacob of his coming, and the old man gathered all his remaining strength and managed to achieve a sitting posture on the side of his bed. He had an important duty to perform, and he was determined to get it done.

He began by reminding Joseph that God had appeared to him twice at Bethel. He repeated to his son the substance of the great promises there made to him. Then he formally adopted Joseph's two sons, Ephraim and Manasseh, as his own, placing them on an equality with Joseph's own brethren. His words were "Now thy two sons, Ephraim and Manasseh, which were born unto thee in the land of Egypt before I came unto thee into Egypt, are mine; as Reuben and Simeon, they shall be mine. And thy issue, which thou begettest after them, shall be thine, and shall be called after the name of their brethren in their inheritance." Thus he put Ephraim and Manasseh into the birthright place forfeited by Reuben. It rightfully belonged to them as the sons of Joseph, who was Rachel's first-born, when it was forfeited by Reuben, Leah's first-born.

It was then that the dying man discerned that Joseph was not alone. Two others were with him whom he could not clearly identify. He asked, "Who are these?" Then followed Joseph's introduction of his sons to their grandfather. Instantly Jacob said, "Bring them . . . unto me, and I will bless them." He kissed and embraced them, saying to Joseph meanwhile, "I had not thought to see thy face: and, lo, God hath shewed me also thy seed."

The Crossed Hands

They knelt before him, Manasseh, the oldest, on the left, where Jacob's right hand would naturally rest upon his head; Ephraim, the younger, on the right, directly in line with Jacob's left hand. Then, surprisingly, the old man crossed his hands, his right resting on Ephraim, his left on Manasseh. In this attitude, before Joseph could speak, he repeated the words, "God, before whom my fathers Abraham and Isaac did walk, the God which fed me all my life long unto this day, the Angel which redeemed me from all evil, bless the lads; and let my name be named on them, and the name of my fathers Abraham and Isaac; and let them grow into a multitude in the midst of the earth."

Joseph was troubled by the position of his father's hands. He knew that Jacob was speaking under special divine guidance, and he wanted no mistake to occur. So he called Jacob's attention to what he had done, and learned quickly that there was no inadvertence about it. "I know it, my son, I know it." What he was doing he did intentionally, carrying out the promptings of God's Spirit, and giving the counsel that God led him to give.

Jacob's time to depart this life came seventeen years after his arrival in Egypt. His sons were around his bed. He had spoken to each of them about their individual future. A silence fell upon them as they solemnly waited for the end to come. He had received from Joseph a pledge that his remains would be carried out of Egypt to Canaan, and there laid to rest in the Cave of Machpelah. Now he lays upon them all the same responsibility that Joseph had assumed regarding his burial in Canaan. Then "he gathered up his feet into the bed, and yielded up the ghost, and was gathered unto his people."

Joseph stepped forward and closed his father's eyes for his last sleep. It is doubtful that he could do this without experiencing the deepest emotion. The memories of the past came rushing back upon him. He thought of his father's indulgent love, of the princely garment, of his father's unfeigned rejoicing in his Egyptian exaltation. This was the first time death had come so close to him. He had been too young to feel deeply his mother's death. He had had seventeen years of unalloyed delight in the companionship of his father. He felt his loss so keenly and the thought of it so overpowered him "that he fell upon his father's face, and wept upon him, and kissed him."

Buried in Canaan

With this burden of grief he took upon himself to make the arrangements for his father's funeral, and the carrying out of his request regarding his burial in Canaan. The body was washed, then wrapped in bands of fine linen, and the days of mourning began. And the mourning for Jacob was a public mourning, as well as a mourning by his family. Pharaoh's permission was sought and obtained for the burial in Canaan.

It was an imposing funeral cortege that made its way out of Egypt. The twelve brothers and their families, excepting only the little ones, were accompanied by an immense array of chariots and horsemen from among the Egyptians. They set out from the land of Goshen to the land of Canaan. When they came to the "threshingfloor of Atad," which cannot now be identified, they halted for seven days to complete the services of mourning. Their lamentations were so great as to strike the attention of the inhabitants, who named the place afterward Abel-Mizraim, the field of mourning of the Egyptians. There the children of Israel left their Egyptian convoy and proceeded alone with the patriarch's remains to lay them reverently in the Cave of Machpelah. Thus they carried out their father's dying request. And Jacob was left to sleep with Abraham and Isaac.

Then Jacob's twelve sons turned away to go back to their children and their homes and flocks in Egypt, and to take up life again without their father. A great career had closed, a strangely checkered career. He had started out in life with little that was attractive. He was naturally tricky, a master of intrigue and deceit. But all this began to change with the Bethel vision. There for the first time he came face to face with God. From that hour began the divine training that developed him as the heir of the covenant. That training culminated in the great experience at Penuel, where his nature was changed and he became the prince of God. After that, while his trials continued, his chastened spirit grew into sainthood, until the career that began in deceit was transformed to excellence and utter devotion to God.

As the brothers returned to Egypt and resumed their usual occupations, the absence of the old father made itself felt in various ways. It awakened in ten of them a sense of uneasiness that now Joseph might feel more inclined to visit upon them the punishment that they knew they deserved for the grave injustice they had worked on him more than a third of a century before. True, he had forgiven them; indeed, had been more than magnanimous toward them, and never seemed to have even a remote thought looking toward retaliation. Their father's restraining hand, however, was now removed. There was nothing to prevent Joseph now from visiting upon them some treatment that would make them smart for the terrible wrong they had done him.

They took their uneasiness at once to Joseph and said, "Thy father did command before he died, saying, So shall ye say unto Joseph, Forgive, I pray thee now, the trespass of thy brethen, and their sin; for they did unto thee evil: and now, we pray thee, forgive the trespass of the servants of the God of thy father."

Again the Dreams Fulfilled

They soon discovered that they had gravely misjudged the character of Joseph. It was not at all the presence of Jacob that had influenced Joseph to forgiveness and kindness. "Joseph wept when they spake unto him." He could not help seeing that he was even yet the object of suspicion and distrust of his brothers. It grieved and hurt him. But his tears constituted the only reproof he addressed to them. Once more they fell down before him, unconsciously fulfilling his old dreams; and he reassured them with the words "Fear not: for am I in the place of God? But as for you, ye thought evil against me; but God meant it unto good, to bring to pass, as it is this day, to save much people alive. Now therefore fear ye not: I will nourish you, and your little ones."

Joseph faithfully carried out that promise, and his brothers no longer doubted him. For the sixty-one years that remained of his life, we have only the record of two verses: "And Joseph dwelt in Egypt, he, and his father's house: and Joseph lived an hundred and ten years. And Joseph saw Ephraim's children of the third generation"—his great-grandchildren—"the children also of Machir the son of Manasseh"—Manasseh's grandchildren—"were brought up upon Joseph's knees." In all he lived ninety-three years in Egypt, eighty of which followed his elevation to the second place in the kingdom. It is likely that he retained to the end of his life the confidence and affection of the royal family, as well as of the nation's people.

CHAPTER 29

"Joseph, When He Died"

THE words that a man speaks as he contemplates death are looked upon as having more than usual significance. The thoughts to which he gives expression before he closes his eyes in that last sleep, just before he passes into eternity, are considered worthy of preservation and quotation. The last thought to which Joseph gave utterance has been preserved for us by Paul, and he describes it in Hebrews 11:22.

"By faith Joseph, when he died, made mention of the departing of the children of Israel; and gave commandment concerning his bones."

Here, in the closing moments of Joseph's life, is a most revealing disclosure of the supreme factor that had sustained and supported him in his whole career, from beginning to end, through all the varied experiences of his life, and which still enabled him to face without uneasiness or fear his approaching death. The record is:

"Joseph took an oath of the children of Israel, saying, God will surely visit you, and ye shall carry up my bones from hence" (Gen. 50:25).

What a wonderfully revealing statement that is! It permits us a glance at the one influence in his life that had sustained him during the hard experiences through which he had passed, and which still sustained him as he faced the future. That future was not uncertain to him. He believed God. He had always believed God. When as a lad God had disclosed to him that there was important work for him to accomplish, a work that was part of God's purpose for His people, Joseph never doubted—though everything about him seemed to contradict it—that God was in control of his destiny and his affairs, and was causing all the outrageous things happening to him to combine for good, and that the outcome would be as God planned it. It was this faith and implicit confidence in God and His overshadowing providence that buoyed him up and carried him through what otherwise would have proved unbearable.

"Joseph . . . made mention of the departing of the children of Israel." It was Joseph who had brought them to Egypt. But he knew when he did it they were not to remain there. Egypt was not their inheritance. Egypt was not their permanent home. Nor was it his. Always it would be to him the land of his affliction. And now as he faced death he spoke of the departing of his people. They were not going to stay. But why should they ever leave? They had grown into a great people there.

God had said they were to leave. And Joseph believed God. God had told his great progenitor, Abraham, "Know of a surety that thy seed shall be a stranger in a land that is not their's, and shall serve them; and they shall afflict them four hundred years; and also that nation, whom they shall serve, will I judge: and afterward shall they come out with a great substance."

God Would Take Them Out

So Joseph knew Israel would leave Egypt. His bones should leave with them. Joseph loved Israel. He had cherished Israel. They were his people. Moreover, they were God's people. God had said to Abraham, "Know of a *surety.*" Just before Joseph died he said, "God will surely visit you." And he repeated it twice. There was certainty here. So he "took an oath" of them that "ye shall carry up my bones from hence."

For Joseph there was another world than this present one. In that other world he lived as truly as he lived in this one. That other world became real to him. It surrounded him at every point. He lived as seeing Him who is invisible. The things that came to him and were hard to bear, that were incomprehensible, were but temporary; and somehow they were advancing the eternal purpose of the One with whom he had to do. It mattered little that he did not understand them. He did not need to understand. He was in the hands of God, and God knew what He was doing, and the reason for it. God would bring things out right. The future was secure, and Joseph lived for that future.

It was this characteristic feature of Joseph's life that is so vividly displayed in his dying charge to his brethren. "God will not leave you in Egypt," he declared. "He will visit you. This I know. He has said so. When He does, see to it that my bones are not left in Egypt. This is not my country. Take my remains with you when God takes you out. I would

186

go with you, and when I wake, I would wake where I belong, in my own land."

It is not difficult to understand why Paul, in listing the heroes of faith in the Epistle to the Hebrews, selected this one act of Joseph's life as the convincing evidence that Joseph should be included in that list of worthies. "By faith Joseph, when he died, made mention of the departing of the children of Israel; and gave commandment concerning his bones." In this Paul discerned the positive evidence that Joseph was a man of profound faith, that he wholly believed the promises of God and longed earnestly for their fulfillment. It was evidence, too, of how little he had felt himself at home in the land of Egypt, though to outward appearance it may have seemed that he had become completely one of its people.

Faith was no new thing to Joseph. It was not something that had come to him in his later years. His remarkable life had been marked by it from the beginning. The world about him, which he could touch and feel and see, was real enough, but it was no more real than the invisible world in which he believed. He could not reach out and touch it; he could and did grasp it by living faith. And it was this faith that not only made the invisible world real to him but also sustained him through all the bludgeonings of what seemed outrageous chance.

This attitude of mind and will, which Joseph constantly manifested toward the invisible world in which he believed, and which made that world so real to him, had been the same from the beginning. From the time when he stood by his grandfather's knee and listened to the life stories of his ancestors and the marvelous dealings of Jehovah with them, through all the providential ordering of his own eventful life, he had not doubted that always and in all circumstances he had been in the hand of the One who sees the end from the beginning and who controls all things in accordance with the counsels of His own will, and makes circumstances answer the far-reaching purposes of His program. This was Joseph's confidence in the beginning when the dreams came to him; this had been his confidence throughout; this would be his confidence to the end; this is still his confidence now that he comes to the end of life and looks into the future. God will visit His people. They would be taken again to their own land. Joseph knew it. And when it came to pass, his bones must not be left in Egypt. They must go home.

The Dying Words of a Great Soul

Joseph's faith led him to trust God, to rely on Him to bring about the fulfillment of His promised word. "They looked unto him, and were lightened: and their faces were not ashamed." It was thus that Joseph lived and was enabled to live through the hard experiences of his life. He knew God was working something out. He was content to wait. And meanwhile it was his faith that exercised its noblest office in his behalf in detaching him from the present and from the circumstances around him. The dying words of this great man of God open a window into his soul and disclose how very little he had felt that he belonged to the order of things in the midst of which he had lived. While he lived, the hope of the inheritance to come burned in his heart as a hidden light, making him an alien, a pilgrim and a stranger, everywhere but on its dear and blessed soil. And now that he was about to bid farewell to life and go to his rest, this too mattered little. His faith operated to detach him from these circumstances, as well as from those that had gone before. His hope penetrated beyond the grave, far into the future. That was all that mattered.

So Joseph's detachment from worldly surroundings is disclosed in these dying words. However, his whole life story discloses something besides this. It shows that his detachment from worldly surroundings, and his absorption with invisible realities and an unseen world, did not make him unfit for or discontented with his earthly environment and responsibilities or disqualify him for great and important service to his fellow men. His detachment did not cut the nerve of, or remove the incentive to, the grandest ministry to mankind, even while his prime interest remained centered on God. His utter absorption in God's plans did not unfit him for his duty in this world while it was preparing him to live in another world. Making God first in all things never operates to make the man of God neglect or ignore or forget his duty to men. When a man loves God with all his soul and strength and mind, he will love his neighbor as himself.

Always Joseph's thoughts had been directed by his faith in God. When the invisible rules in men's lives it must be through their thoughts. Certitude such as that comes by faith alone. That is what faith can and will do for any man—make God real, make the unseen world real.

Moreover, Joseph's faith, as we have seen, directed and controlled his desires. When the unseen rules in a man's heart, it becomes not merely the object of certain knowledge; it becomes also the object of his dearest wishes. It ceases to be doubtful, dim, uncertain, but becomes infinitely desirable. In comparison with it, all things else become insignificant.

A life detached from this world and fixed upon the unseen holds, as we have seen in the case of Joseph, innumerable benefits. A man who lives for future and remote objectives that are of the utmost desirability to him, and upon which his heart is fixed, will be a better man than the man who is living for today alone, living in and for the present. So living, enduring as seeing the invisible, he unconsciously subjects himself to a mental and moral discipline that becomes of infinite benefit to him.

Such living, too, will bring about a subtle change of character that will be highly beneficial. Whatever causes a man to live in the past and in the future elevates him. High above other men is the man to whom all the past is a disclosure of God—a revelation of His providence with Calvary at its center—and all the future a fellowship with Christ and joys forevermore in the world to come.

What Otherworldliness Does

Living by such a faith as Joseph exhibited does more. It changes the center of a man's interest from this world to another, from earth to heaven. That is the never-changing work of faith, of otherworldliness. Abraham, we are told, "sojourned . . . as in a strange country, dwelling in tabernacles . . . : for he looked for a city which hath foundations, whose builder and maker is God" (Heb. 11:8-10).

It should be emphasized anew that such a faith as Joseph possessed and exercised does not make a man indifferent to his duties in this world. That is the world's sneer. Joseph's life refutes that sneer. He was faithful and diligent in all his duties. He was energetic and deeply loyal to his masters. He remained a true Hebrew all his life. But that did not cause him to abandon or neglect Pharaoh's service. He lived by hope, and by his faith in the unseen. This, instead of making him an indifferent worker, made him a better one by the passing day. He plainly believed that the more diligently and selflessly and devotedly he applied himself to his duties and responsibilities, the more surely the God whom he served would bring to pass the realization of his great dreams;

God would fulfill His own divine purpose. To live for and with respect to the world to come does not unfit any man for the present world. To live constantly as a citizen of the celestial world makes any man a better citizen while he remains in this world. The faith in Joseph's heart kept him all his life diligently doing things of the moment, whether as a slave, as a prisoner, or while administering the affairs of a great empire.

Indeed, as in Joseph's case, the duties and responsibilities that belong to a man in this life take on a greater importance when he realizes the reality of the unseen, and lives his life here with respect to the life there. Then the occurrences and circumstances of the present life, shot through as they are with disappointment and grief, become less in their power to trouble us, while the work and duties of the present life assume a larger importance as they become preparations for what is coming, if done with scrupulous care and diligence.

Elevated Above the World

Thus faith such as Joseph possessed, instead of enervating a man for work in this world, rather energizes him for any sort of work he may be required to do. Look again at that muster roll of the heroes of faith in Hebrews 11, and mark the variety of levels of human life represented there. They were all made by their faith, fitted for their tasks and delivered from the snare inherent in their respective callings. Their faith elevated them above the world, and consequently put them in a position to come down on their work with more powerful strokes of duty.

We who live in this gospel age possess a larger and clearer revelation of God than did Joseph. It should and may develop in us a faith in all that God has promised—a faith even beyond that of this ancient patriarch whose story has so thrilled us—so that we too may have his calmness, his assurance, his firmness, in the developments of our lives. Then the same power that held him true and steady and unmoved in all circumstances will work in us not only the same detachment and the same energy in life but the same devotion to God under all conditions; it will provide for us the same clear light and hope in the approach of death.

"Joseph . . . gave commandment concerning his bones." He wanted them removed from Egypt. The dying prime minister of Egypt could have given commandment that a magnificent monument be prepared as the permanent resting place for his bones. He could have had his body mummified and a great pyramid built for it. Other great men of Egypt had given such commandments. And their monuments still remain. Joseph wanted his bones removed from Egypt and taken to another land, the Land of Promise.

Why Not a Great Pyramid?

Why? What moved his mind so that he wanted his bones in Canaan rather than in Egypt? Why was burial in Egypt rejected and burial in Canaan commanded? Joseph had been a ruler in Egypt. The presence of his tomb there would have been a permanent testimony to the great work he had done for the nation, as well as to the faithfulness of the God of the Hebrews. It was the true God who had interpreted Pharaoh's dream. Joseph said so. It was the true God who had provided the plan that saved Egypt. A grand monument to Joseph in Egypt, some permanent memorial, perhaps a majestic pyramid where his bones could lie, would serve a double purpose in perpetuating his memory while at the same time honoring the true God. In that pyramid Joseph's body could sleep its long sleep in mummy form beside the famous Pharaohs of the centuries. Thus the peoples of the land where he had been such a great earthly success, as well as all visitors from other lands, would be provided with a reminder of that success, and perhaps be pointed to the true God, who had brought it about.

None of these considerations moved Egypt's great prime minister when the time came for him to look into the future. They were of little interest to him. When he contemplated death, Joseph's faith brought to him a vision of something other, something greater, something far more desirable, than monuments, than pyramids, than human acclaim.

As Joseph reached the end of his earthly life he had not lost his confidence that the God of his fathers would carry out His promise to Abraham, Isaac, and Jacob—the promise that He would give them the Land of Promise for an everlasting possession. That promise was not yet fulfilled. They all slept in the Promised Land. Joseph believed they would be raised from the dead and enter into the possession of the land, as God had promised. He wanted his bones carried back to Canaan where he could sleep along with his progenitors, so that on the great day when Abraham, Isaac, and Jacob were brought from their tombs to enter upon their long-promised inheritance, he too would be with them in that resurrection, and with them share in the possession of the Promised Land.

Life Without End in the Eternal Land of Promise

So Joseph, when he came to die, was not thinking of the things of time—monuments, memorials, pyramids—or of the things of Egypt and earthly glory. His eye penetrated by faith into the things of eternity, into the glories of the resurrection, of life without end in the dear land of the promise, associated with his father, his grandfather, and his revered great-grandfather Abraham. What were earthly glories and renown compared with the things that God had promised?

Thus Joseph, when about to die, made mention concerning his bones, because the resurrection from the dead was very real to him. He was not going to remain dead. He was going to live again. He wanted no monument. He was looking forward to life, life in the Land of Promise. Abraham was awaiting the resurrection there, as were Isaac and Jacob. He would rest there with them and rise with them in a triumphant resurrection over death and the grave. What a glorious way to die!

And so Joseph came to the end of his long and exalted life. Through it all the God of his fathers had sustained and guided him. Through the widely varied vicissitudes of his colorful life—seventeen years as a carefree lad in his father's encampment; ten years in Egyptian slavery; three years in a dungeon; and eighty years as lord of all Egypt, and elder statesman, revered as the savior of the nation—he had trusted God. And God never failed him. Always to Joseph He was Jehovah-jireh, the One who will provide in all circumstances, the One who will always "see to it." Circumstances were always changing with Joseph. God did not change. Always He was the same.

Joseph died. And that was *not* the end of him. For he died as he had lived, in tune with the Infinite. God had sent a man. In the vast, timeless, endless eternity to come, the God whom Joseph loved and served will take this faithful servant to Himself to be with Him in unbroken harmony and unending fellowship, world without end.